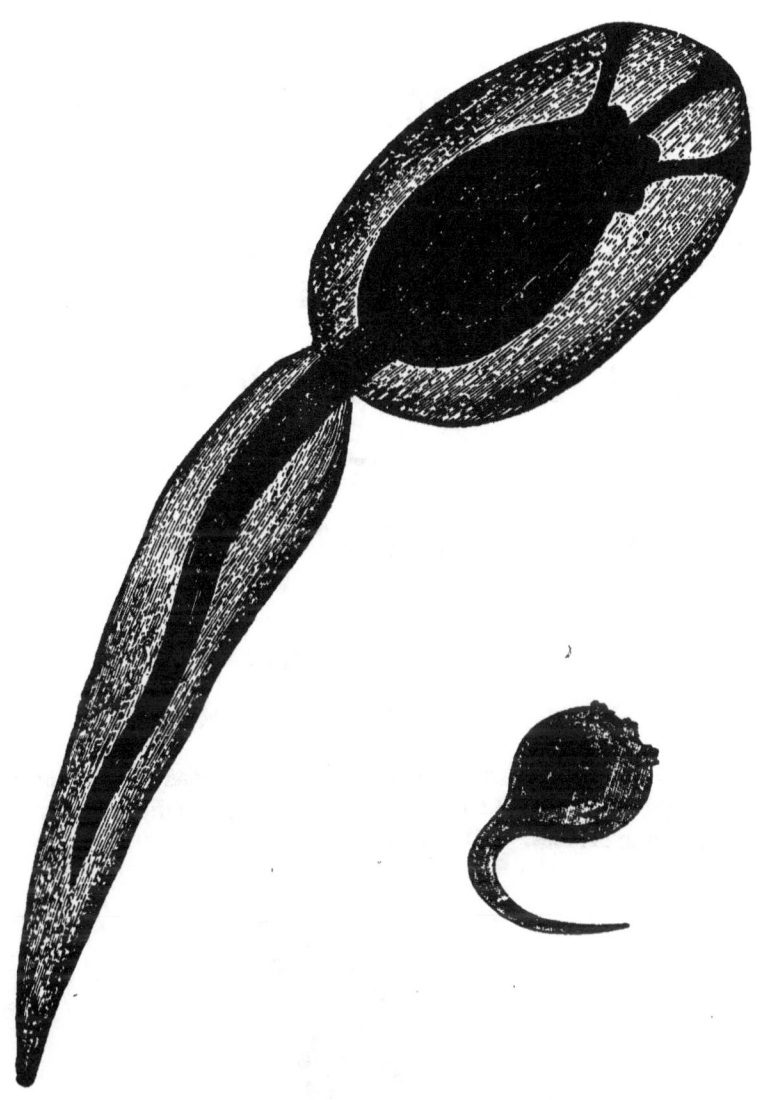

ASCIDIAN TADPOLES.

THE LARGER FIGURE HIGHLY MAGNIFIED.

Given that the reader may form some idea of man's very remote ancestors, according to Mr. Darwin. See page 13.

HOMO versus DARWIN:

A

JUDICIAL EXAMINATION

OF

STATEMENTS RECENTLY PUBLISHED BY MR. DARWIN
REGARDING

"THE DESCENT OF MAN."

BY

W. P. LYON, B.A.

───────▶
SECOND EDITION.
───────

"Ascidians are marine creatures permanently attached to a support. They hardly appear like animals, and consist of a simple, tough, leathery sac, with two small projecting orifices."—MR. DARWIN.

AN ASCIDIAN.

LONDON:
HAMILTON, ADAMS, AND CO., 32, PATERNOSTER ROW.

HENRY BLACKLOCK & CO.,
PRINTERS,
ALLEN STREET, GOSWELL ROAD, LONDON, E.C.

ERRATA.

Page 135 *line* 5 *for* So *read* To
Page 135 *line* 6 *for* man. *read* man,
Page 143 *line* 23 *for* changes, *read* changed,

PREFACE.

At the beginning of this year the reading classes of England were all, more or less, in a state of expectancy, their attention being fixed on Mr. Darwin, who was known to be engaged in bringing out a work which was to mark a new era in Natural Science. It was confidently believed by many that he had in his possession facts which would enable him to establish his favourite hypothesis on a sure basis, and lay all his opponents, whether men or systems, defeated in the dust.

The work at length appeared, and was eagerly read by thousands throughout our land. There is no difficulty in getting through the two volumes of which it is composed, for they abound in facts gathered from that most interesting field of enquiry—Natural History; and where facts fail him, Mr. Darwin is able, in their stead, to present suppositions quite as interesting, and perhaps even more startling.

But to the mind of a serious reader this is all that can be obtained from its perusal, for Mr. Darwin's style of reasoning is eminently unsatisfactory. One by one, with cool indifference, he throws overboard, not only Christianity, but also the tried and sure methods of the inductive philosophy of Bacon, which would have sunk his light craft—and along with these the first axioms of logic and common sense.

As a remonstrance against this unwarrantable outrage on religion and philosophy, as well as on true science, the present volume has been penned. The writer has presented his thoughts on the main questions raised by Mr. Darwin in the form of a judicial enquiry, in order thus, more clearly, and in a more lively manner, to put before his readers the important points at issue, and also to bring Mr. Darwin face to face with those well-known and acknowledged principles of investigation which he is only too ready to ignore.

September 27th, 1871.

NOTE TO THE SECOND EDITION.—A fresh illustration of the argument, derived from the differences that exist between different species, in the blood and in the minute structures of the body, will be found in pages 154—156 of the present edition.

January 30th, 1872.

CONTENTS.

The Case is referred for arbitration to Lord C.

FIRST DAY'S SITTING.—Opening of the Case.

PAGE

Homo states his ground of complaint—Mr. Darwin traces man's pedigree from the tadpole-like offspring of ancient Ascidians through fishes, amphibians, reptiles, and the lower mammals, to Old World monkeys; from thence, through a long series of now vanished forms, to man—Ascidians and their larvæ—All intermediate forms between ape and man extinct — Professor Huxley knows of no new species having been originated by selection—Mr. Darwin's former belief in the possibility of black bears being changed into creatures like whales—The historic period refuses its help to Mr. Darwin—Geology unable to supply him with the missing links ...   9—32

SECOND DAY'S SITTING.—Mr. Darwin's Defence.

Discussion on evidence adduced by Mr. Darwin of man's descent from some lower form—Bodily structure—Embryology—Rudiments—The panniculus—The external ear—M.B. ears—The third eyelid—Sense of smell—How man has ceased to inherit the hairy coat of his progenitors   ...   .   32—58

THIRD DAY'S SITTING.—Mr. Darwin's Defence. *(Cont.)*

Discussion on rudiments continued—Occasional long hairs of the eyebrow—Lanugo—Wisdom teeth—The great canine teeth of our progenitors used for tearing their enemies—Mr. Darwin's mistakes—How did man lose his tail?—Has a Creator never intervened?   ...   59—76

FOURTH DAY'S SITTING.—Mr. Darwin's Defence. *(Cont.)*

Mr. Darwin's account of the way in which an ape-like creature may change insensibly into man—It lives less on trees and more on the ground—Finds it convenient to become biped and erect—Hands suitable for climbing trees, not suitable for hurling stones or spears—Hence an ape's hands change in the human direction, and also its feet—Africa, the supposed country of man's progenitors, abounds with dangerous beasts—How man's progenitors may have escaped them when losing their brute-like powers—They may, however, have inhabited some safer country—The brain of man in comparison with the brain of the ape ... ... 77—88

FIFTH DAY'S SITTING.—Close of Mr. Darwin's Defence.

Man's mental and moral powers—The lowest savages resemble us in the mental faculty—Points on which man is said to differ essentially from the lower animals—Capacity for progressive improvement—The manufacture of tools—The use of fire—The orang's first step in architecture—Language—General ideas, abstraction, &c.—Sense of beauty—Belief in God—Religion—Reasoning power of Mr. Darwin's dog—Can a dog distinguish between moral right and wrong?—Mr. Darwin's views of conscience and the moral sense—The new and strange morality to which his principles lead—How family murder might have been a sacred duty—Sympathy for the weak and helpless causes a degeneration of the race of man—Probable effect of Mr. Darwin's principles on the rising generation—Visionary Speculations—The mystery of life ... ... 89—133

SIXTH DAY'S SITTING. Summing up by Lord C.

Ancient and more recent speculations on the origin of the universe and of man—No views hitherto put forth on Evolution have been established—Mr. Darwin's style of argument—He now admits the existence of unknown agencies—Past history and present experience against him—Many living species have remained unchanged during 3000 generations—The sterility of cross breeds—Geology—Professor Huxley and the pedigree of the horse—Professor Owen—Rudiments—A wonderful transformation—Mr. Darwin's ape excepted, monkeys have remained monkeys for millions of ages—The mental faculty—The Darwinian morality—What it involves, practical atheism—The dogma of separate creations not taught in Scripture—Darwinism and Christianity irreconcilable—Lord C.'s award—Homo's proposal for a settlement of the case—Lord C.'s closing advice to Mr. Darwin ... ...134—155

HOMO versus DARWIN.

FIRST DAY'S SITTING.

IT having been agreed, on the recommendation of the Judge before whom this case was to have been tried, to refer it for arbitration to Lord C——, one of the ablest of English Jurists, that the evidence on which Mr. Darwin's statements rest might be thoroughly sifted, and also that the Plaintiff and Defendant should each speak for himself; on the opening of the Court, Homo, was called on to state his ground of complaint, and spoke as follows:—

My case, my Lord, may be stated in a very few words. It is well known to your Lordship, and will not be denied by the Defendant, that, during many centuries, it has been acknowledged that my first ancestors derived existence directly from a Divine source, and were, therefore, in a very intelligible sense, the offspring of God. There are ancient documents with which your Lordship is familiar, and which many of the most powerful intellects our country has produced have regarded as divinely true, in which such is certified to be the origin of my race. This sentiment is confirmed by the traditions of all civilized nations, and it is generally admitted by men of philosophic mind that my nature bears on itself evident traces of its alliance with the Divine.

I have to complain, then, that the Defendant, following in the track of some recent naturalists, has lately published a work entitled "The Descent of Man," in which he affirms that I am "certainly descended from some ape-like creature." "Man," he says, "is descended from a hairy quadruped, furnished with a tail and pointed ears, probably arboreal in its habits, and an inhabitant of the old world." (Vol. ii. p. 389.) "The early progenitors of man," he says again, "were no doubt well covered with hair, both sexes having beards; their ears were pointed and capable of movement; and their bodies were provided with a tail, having the proper muscles. . . . The males were provided with great canine teeth, which served them as formidable weapons." (Vol. i. pp. 206, 207.)

But this is not all, my Lord. Mr. Darwin further affirms that my most ancient progenitors were creatures resembling the larvæ, or young of Ascidians—the Ascidians being scarcely animals at all. They are classed by some naturalists among the worms, while their young resemble tadpoles. Mr. Darwin thus affirms that I am descended from a tadpole, and am, in short, the offspring of a worm!

I have to complain, my Lord, that, in maintaining such to be my origin, Mr. Darwin entirely ignores the general sentiment and belief of my race regarding it, and also the historical and philosophical evidence on which it rests, and that he takes occasion, from some points in my bodily structure in which it resembles those of the lower animals, to affirm that I am sprung from the same stock with them, and differ from them merely by virtue of processes which he calls "Natural Selection" and "Sexual Selection." He thus degrades me from being a creature made by the Divine hand and bearing traces of the Divine image, to be merely a more perfectly developed animal, and allied, rather to the apes and monkeys of the present day, than to the Almighty Creator of all things. I have to complain, my Lord, that this attempt of Mr. Darwin to give me a brutish origin, not only degrades me in my own estimation, but is calculated to have an injurious effect on my youthful offspring. Let them but be taught that they are the relatives of apes and monkeys, instead of being the offspring of God, and that their most ancient progenitor was a tadpole and a worm, and it will take away from them one of the most powerful motives to act a rational, worthy, and noble part on the great stage of human life.

Lord C. As I understand the matter, then, the head and front of Mr. Darwin's offending is, that he affirms you to be descended from a hairy quadruped, and more remotely from some creature like a tadpole, instead of having been created immediately by the Divine Being. You also complain of Mr. Darwin's statements as being not only untrue, but also offensive and libellous, and likely to exert an injurious influence on the youthful portion of your race.

Homo. Precisely so, my Lord. He affirms that " it is only our natural prejudice, and that arrogance which made our forefathers declare that they were descended from demi-gods, which leads us to demur to this conclusion." (Vol. i. p. 33.)

Lord C. The conclusion certainly is not a flattering one. But I should like Mr. Darwin himself to state the view regarding our descent which he is endeavouring to propagate.

Darwin. My Lord, "I give" to man "a pedigree of prodigious length," if not "of noble quality." "The most ancient progenitors in the kingdom of the Vertebrata at which we are able to obtain an obscure glance, apparently consisted of a group of marine animals, resembling the larvæ of existing Ascidians. These animals probably gave rise to a group of fishes, as lowly organized as the Lancelet; and from these the Ganoids and other fishes like the Lepidosiren, must have been developed. From such fish a very small advance would carry us on to the amphibians. . . . Birds and reptiles were once intimately connected together, and the Monotremata now, in a slight degree, connect mammals with reptiles. But no one can at present say by what line of descent the three higher and related classes, namely, mammals, birds, and reptiles, were derived from either of the two lower vertebrate classes, namely, amphibians and fishes. In the class of mammals the steps are not difficult to conceive which led from the ancient Monotremata to the ancient Marsupials; and from these to the early progenitors of the placental animals. We may thus ascend to the Lemuridæ; and the interval is not wide from these to the Simiadæ. The Simiadæ then branched off into two great stems, the New World and the Old World monkeys, and from the latter, at a remote period, man, the wonder and glory of the universe, proceeded. . . . . If a single link in this chain had never existed, man would not have been what he now is. Unless we wilfully close our eyes, we may, with our present knowledge, approximately recognize our parentage, nor need we feel ashamed of it." (Vol. i. pp. 212, 213.)

Homo. I hope, my Lord, that Mr. Darwin will not charge me with wilfully closing my eyes because I feel unable to recognize my parentage either in monkeys or tadpoles.

Darwin. I beg Homo's pardon, my Lord; but, like Pilate of old, " what I have written, I have written."

Lord C. Perhaps Homo is not yet sufficiently advanced in knowledge to be able to make the recognition in question. I must confess that I find myself in a similar predicament.

I never heard of these "ancient progenitors" of ours—the Ascidians—till now. Will Mr. Darwin inform me what Ascidians are?

Darwin. Ascidians, my Lord, are "invertebrate, hermaphrodite, marine creatures permanently attached to a support. They hardly appear like animals, and consist of a simple, tough, leathery sac, with two small projecting orifices... They have recently been placed by some naturalists among the Vermes or worms. Their larvæ somewhat resemble tadpoles in shape, and have the power of swimming freely about." (Vol. i. p. 205.)

Homo. Mr. Darwin, my Lord, has not supplied us with an engraving of an Ascidian in his book, but here is one which I have been allowed to copy from Professor Huxley's "Introduction to the Classification of Animals." The Professor says, "They look very much like double-necked jars. At first sight you might hardly suspect the animal nature of one of these organisms, when freshly taken from the sea; but if you touch it, the stream of water which it squirts out of each aperture reveals the existence of a great contractile power within." Of the two apertures, A serves as a mouth; B is the anal aperture, and C the base of attachment, by which it fastens itself to a bit of seaweed or to a rock. This is called a "Solitary Ascidian," because it exists by itself; others are called "Social," "Aggregate," or "Compound Ascidians," because they exist in groups, a number of them being united into a mass.

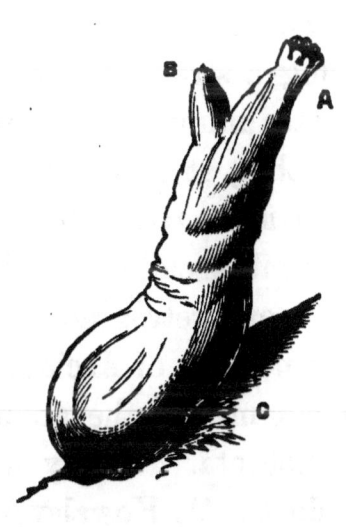

Lord C. Foreshadowing, perhaps, the family groups of their remote human posterity!

Homo. Mr. Darwin, my Lord, does not tell us whether ancient Ascidians were social or not. It is their degenerate posterity we are now looking at. Here (see *Frontispiece*) is another engraving, showing the larvæ of Ascidians. The large one, from the "Penny Encyclopædia," is highly magnified, and shows the creature when newly hatched. The smaller one is from "Chambers' Encyclopædia." These authorities state that "they resemble tadpoles in shape, and swim by means of a vibratile tail, which they shake off when they quit the larva state and assume the sessile (sitting or fixed) condition."

Lord C. On what ground do you affirm, Mr. Darwin, that we human beings are descended from creatures such as these?

Darwin. "If we may rely on Embryology," my Lord, "which has always proved the safest guide in classification, we have at last gained a clue to the source whence the Vertebrata have been derived." It has lately been discovered that "the larvæ of Ascidians are related to the Vertebrata, in their manner of development, in the relative position of the nervous system, and in possessing a structure closely like the *chorda dorsalis* of vertebrate animals. . . . We should thus be justified in believing that, at an extremely remote period, a group of animals existed resembling in many respects the larvæ of our present Ascidians, which diverged into two great branches—the one retrograding in development, and producing the present class of Ascidians, the other rising to the crown and summit of the animal kingdom by giving birth to the Vertebrata." I may add that "some observations lately made by M. Kowalevsky, since confirmed by Professor Kuppfer," led to this discovery, which will be one of "extraordinary interest, if still further extended, as I hear from M. Kowalevsky, in Naples, he has now effected." (Vol. i. pp. 205, 206.)

Homo. Pray observe, my Lord, the remarkable mental agility of Mr. Darwin. To reach his desired conclusion, he leaps, at a bound, over all the recognized laws of reasoning. First, he tells us that a foreign gentleman lately made "some observations," which observations, it appears, another foreign gentleman confirmed. Mr. Darwin then hears from the first foreign gentleman that he has "further extended" those observations. We are then unhesitatingly told that those observations have led to the discovery that the tadpole-like Ascidians of the present day—which, for brevity's sake, we may, I presume, henceforth speak of simply as tadpoles—are "related in descent to the Vertebrata." Another element of uncertainty is then introduced into the argument. "*If*," says Mr. Darwin, "*if* we may rely on Embryology... we have at last gained a clue to the source whence the Vertebrata have been derived." From these hypothetical premises—a portion of which only I have detailed—he draws the conclusion, "We should thus be justified in believing" that we are descended from "a group of animals resembling the larvæ of our present Ascidians." Now, even were these premises of Mr. Darwin satisfactorily proved, my Lord, they do not justify his conclusion. No reputable man of science would dream of inferring from them that there was an ancient race of tadpoles more respectable than any now in existence, and that these ancient tadpoles were the progenitors of man on the one hand, and of the degenerate tadpoles of these days on the other. If such reasoning be valid, why, then, one might undertake to prove that Tenterden steeple is the cause of the Goodwin Sands!

Lord C. You had better, Homo, let Mr. Darwin reason

in his own way. Of course, you are not bound by his conclusions.

Homo. But is it not necessary, my Lord, that the facts—so called—on which he bases his hypothesis, should be verified? Mr. Darwin says himself that "false facts are highly injurious to the progress of science." (Vol. ii. p. 385.) Can the unverified observations then, of two foreign gentlemen, afford a sufficient ground for the affirmation that the root of human nature is to be found in a tadpole; or that a worm, by a numberless succession of improvements, has developed into man?

Lord C. If, for the sake of argument, you will accept as facts what Mr. Darwin advances as facts, we shall be the better able to test the value of his hypothesis. Mr. Darwin, I am sure, would not knowingly put forward false statements.

Homo. I do not suppose he would, my Lord, for exposure would be certain; but it is quite possible that over-fondness for his hypothesis, the child of his own brain, might make him less careful than he should be in accepting the statements of others. Indeed, he repeatedly errs in this direction, as I could easily show your Lordship. But I am quite willing to adopt your Lordship's suggestion. We shall, for the sake of argument, suppose Mr. Darwin's facts to be real facts. But I shall take the liberty, when I think it needful, of pointing out their unsatisfactory character.

Lord C. You will be quite right in doing so. To return then to our argument. Mr. Darwin, it appears, maintains that our line of descent, if traced backwards, as far as he can reach, would lead us to creatures somewhat resembling in shape the tadpoles of the present day.

Darwin. What I say, my Lord, is this: "The most ancient progenitors in the kingdom of the Vertebrata (to which kingdom man belongs), at which we are able to obtain an obscure glance, apparently consisted of a group of marine animals, resembling the larvæ of existing Ascidians."

Lord C. And Ascidians "have been recently placed," you say, "by some naturalists, among the Vermes or worms." Job, then, would almost seem to have anticipated your hypothesis when he said to the worm, "Thou art my mother." There is, however, this difference; Job meant it figuratively, you mean it literally and in reality.

Darwin. Precisely so, my Lord; and thus, as I have said, "we approximately recognize our parentage, nor need we feel ashamed of it."

Lord C. Well, that is a matter of taste—I should rather say, perhaps, of feeling or sentiment.

Homo. I should say, my Lord, the imagination has a good deal to do with it.

Lord C. We proceed now to look at the evidence. Is it the case, then, Mr. Darwin, that in endeavouring to work out the conclusion you have arrived at, you take no account of evidence hostile to it, derived from such sources as Homo has referred to—I mean such sources as revelation, tradition, the reasonings of philosophers, &c. ?

Darwin. My Lord, I am a naturalist, and I follow the line of evidence with which my favourite study has made me familiar.

Lord C. But is it wise to ignore other lines of evidence? In courts of law we feel bound to take note of evidence, from whatever source it may come. It seems to me that the true spirit of philosophy, which is just a sincere love of truth—would lead you to pursue a similar course. How can you justify yourself, in so serious a matter, in pooh-poohing evidence which some of the greatest of your countrymen have thought conclusive on the other side?

Homo. Pardon me, my Lord, but I think that, in wilfully

closing his eyes to evidence that may be brought from other sources, Mr. Darwin makes himself, so far, like a horse when we have put on its blinkers, and which, therefore, can see only in one direction. There is just this difference; Mr. Darwin makes his own blinkers and puts them on himself. He is thus disabled from seeing in any line of observation but that of Natural History. He has, moreover, become so blinded by the unnatural use he makes of his eyes, that he cannot see very clearly with them anywhere.

Lord C. You must speak respectfully of Mr. Darwin, Homo.

Homo. I beg your Lordship's pardon if I have transgressed. I desire to cherish every kind feeling towards Mr. Darwin, but hope, at the same time, that I may not be prevented from fully speaking out my mind.

Lord C. I understand, then, that Mr. Darwin thinks the evidence which he brings from Natural History as to our descent from a hairy quadruped, and, more remotely, from creatures resembling the larvæ of Ascidians, to be so conclusive as quite to set aside any evidence to the contrary that might be brought from other sources, and, indeed, to render it unworthy of any notice whatever. I understand also that Mr. Darwin does not suppose man to have been immediately produced by this hairy quadruped, but to be merely his remote descendant; that other races—each succeeding one, I presume, being less ape-like and more human-like—intervened; and that each of these races, through the power of Natural Selection, produced a fresh race, less like the original, till at length the last of them produced man.

Darwin. There must, my Lord, have been "a series of forms graduating insensibly from some ape-like creature to man as he now exists." (Vol. i. p. 235.)

Lord C. Do any of these intervening "series of forms," then, survive?

Darwin. None of them, my Lord. Indeed, "the great break in the organic chain between man and his nearest allies, which cannot be bridged over by any extinct or living species, has often been advanced as a grave objection to the belief that man is descended from some lower form." (Vol. i. p. 200.)

Lord C. I do not wonder at that, for, as the race of man has proved hardy enough to survive, one would think that some, at least, of his ancestral races would have proved as hardy as himself. But perhaps you suppose that, when the series that has ended in man branched away from the stem of the Old World monkeys, all the members in each successive series were travelling gradually towards the goal of humanity, so that a time at length came, when each surviving mother in the last series found herself strangely producing man.

Darwin. My Lord, will you kindly observe that I spoke of "a series of forms, graduating *insensibly* from some ape-like creature to man."

Homo. I should say, my Lord, that, if this "graduating" process ever took place, it was a very sensible process, though "insensibly" performed.

Lord C. Mr. Darwin's meaning is clear enough. He means by "insensibly" that each step in the series of changes by which, at length, ape became man, was trivial in itself, though the whole combined has produced the result which we now see. But I wish to learn from Mr. Darwin, whether he supposes that each step in this series of changes which he thinks resulted in the production of man, was taken by *all* the mothers belonging to each series of forms. Or, I may put it differently. After the line that produced man had branched away from the Old World monkeys, did all the mothers in each succeeding "series of forms" produce offspring "insensibly" in advance of themselves; or was it only *some* of the mothers that did so? This question is important, for, if only *some* of the mothers produced offspring in advance of themselves, then we might inquire what became of the descendants of the other mothers.

Darwin. You have an answer to that question, my Lord, in my reference to "the great break in the organic chain between man and his nearest allies, which cannot be bridged over by any extinct or living species." This implies clearly enough, that, of the intermediate species between man and his nearest allies, all have become extinct.

Lord C. I quite understand that, Mr. Darwin. But if you could have said that *all* the mothers in each succeeding series produced an offspring insensibly in advance of themselves, your hypothesis would have accounted for each successive series having become extinct. Suppose, for example, that while *some* of the mothers in each succeeding series produced offspring in advance of themselves—or, if it suit you better, only *one* of the mothers—the other mothers, being either not so thoughtful, or not so ambitious, produced offspring in their own exact image and likeness, it seems but fair to suppose further that some of those intermediate series of forms would have survived, and that we should thus have about us, at the present day, races of creatures graduating, if not "insensibly," yet clearly and unmistakeably towards man. Or again; if there were "a series of forms graduating insensibly toward man," the number of forms, in that series of forms, must have been enormous; the more insensible the process, the greater the number of forms. Now, I want to know how you account for the fact—for a fact it must be, if your hypothesis be true—that each of these numerous intermediate series of forms has become extinct. Why have we no species of living creature half-way between ape and man? Why is not the vast gap filled up by two or three, or more of these supposed numerous intermediate forms?

Darwin. That, my Lord, " has often been advanced as a grave objection to the belief that man is descended from some lower form, but this objection will not appear of much weight to those who, convinced by general reasons, believe in the general principle of evolution. Breaks incessantly occur in all parts of the series, some being wide, sharp, and defined, others less so in various degrees; as between the orang and its nearest allies—between the Tarsius and the other Lemuridæ . . . but all these breaks depend merely on the number of related forms that have become extinct." (Vol. i. pp. 200, 201.)

Lord C. I have been arguing that, as these supposed related forms graduated "insensibly" from ape to man, their number must have been very great, but you seem to make no difficulty of the circumstance of their all having become extinct.

Darwin. It is certainly no difficulty whatever to me, my Lord. "At some future period, not very distant as measured by centuries, the civilized races of man will almost certainly exterminate and replace throughout the world the savage races. At the same time the anthropomorphous (man-shaped) apes, as Professor Schaaffhausen has remarked, will no doubt be exterminated. The break will then be rendered wider." (Vol. i. p. 201.)

Homo. What Mr. Darwin says, my Lord, sounds very learned, but it does not meet the difficulty suggested.

Lord C. It certainly does not. I can understand that civilized man may, in the course of time, exterminate savage man and man-shaped apes, but I cannot so easily understand why the numerous related forms between ape and man, if they ever really existed, should all have perished. So far as I understand Mr. Darwin's principle of Natural Selection, it is the process by which the stronger races, and those best fitted to succeed, are preserved in the struggle for life. According to Natural Selection, therefore, each of the successive races of man's progenitors, from the "hairy quadruped" on to man himself, must have been better fitted to maintain its position in the world than any which preceded it. We find, however, that, while many monkey tribes survive, all of these have perished. Here, as it seems to me, is an exceedingly weak point in Mr. Darwin's reasoning. According to his hypothesis, the fittest should survive; according to his facts, the fittest have perished!

Homo. In reply to your Lordship's remarks, Mr. Darwin would doubtless say that the fittest have *survived;* that each successive race of man's progenitors, being superior to that which preceded it, exterminated it, and eventually took its place. This, my Lord, is Natural Selection, *i.e.* "the survival of the fittest."

Lord C. I quite understand that Mr. Darwin would say so, but the statement does not carry conviction with it. Many of the supposed races of man's progenitors must have been greatly in advance of any surviving species of monkey.

Homo. My Lord, I defy Mr. Darwin to prove that any one of these numerous related forms between man and ape, which he says were originated by Natural Selection, and have become extinct, ever existed, unless in his own imagination. It is all very fine to talk of the "general principle of evolution," but let Mr. Darwin, or any one of those who say they believe in evolution, point to a single, clear, and unmistakeable instance of it. Professor Huxley, who tells us that he has "assuredly no bias against Mr. Darwin's views," distinctly states that "there is no instance in which a group of animals, having all the characters exhibited by species in nature, has ever been originated by selection, whether natural or artificial."

Lord C. What say you, Mr. Darwin, to this statement of Professor Huxley?

Darwin. I cannot contradict it, my Lord; but, in the passage quoted, Professor Huxley is referring to a former work of mine on THE ORIGIN OF SPECIES BY MEANS OF NATURAL SELECTION; or, *The Preservation of Favoured Races in the Struggle for Life*. But Homo should have stated what follows. The Professor adds, "We will go so far as to express our belief that experiments, conducted by a skilful physiologist, would very probably result in obtaining the desired production in a comparatively few years."

Homo. The Professor is a skilful physiologist, my Lord; let him then try the experiment. I shall willingly wait a few years to see the result. But numberless experiments have unquestionably been made already. Mr. Darwin has no doubt tried some himself—unsuccessfully of course, else we should not yet have heard the end of it. Let him try again. To originate a new species would confer immortality on any physiologist. But I suspect that like will persist in producing its like, in spite of naturalists and their experiments.

Lord C. Pray do not get excited, Homo; keep calm.

Homo. I cannot help it, my Lord, when I find myself led on such a wild-goose chase after ancestors that never existed, and that would be no credit to me if they had.

Lord C. Do not be too confident; perhaps Mr. Darwin may find one of them for you yet. As I understand the case so far, then, it stands thus. Professor Huxley, with assuredly no bias against Mr. Darwin's views—indeed, it is well known that his bias is in favour of them—yet declares that no instance can be adduced in which a distinct species of animal has been originated by what you call Natural Selection. It may be possible, the Professor believes, that a skilful physiologist might in a few years succeed in originating a distinct species, but it has not yet been done. Probably, as Homo suggests, experiments have been made for the purpose of obtaining this desired production, but hitherto without success. Nature has, as yet, proved too stubborn for the physiologist. Nor is there any clear and distinct proof that any species has ever been originated by Natural Selection. No instance can be pointed to in which the thing has certainly and unmistakeably been accomplished. Those who "believe in the general principle of evolution" are "convinced by general reasons," not by tangible and indisputable facts.

Darwin. My Lord, "a large number of naturalists admit that species are the modified descendants of other species; and this especially holds good with the younger and rising naturalists. The greater number accept the agency of Natural Selection; though some urge, whether with justice the future must decide, that I have greatly overrated its importance. Of the older and honoured chiefs in natural science, many, unfortunately, are still opposed to evolution in every form." (Vol. i. pp. 1, 2.)

Lord C. This is certainly "unfortunate" for your hypothesis; but whether it be unfortunate for the interests of truth, the future, as you say, must decide. The point, however, on which I am now remarking is this; you have absolutely no facts as a basis for your hypothesis. It is supported, as I understand, not by facts, but by "general reasons."

Darwin. Those "general reasons," my Lord, are based on facts.

Lord C. Quite so, Mr. Darwin. Your book, I am well aware, is full of facts. Of course, you reason from those facts, and endeavour to build up your hypothesis on them; but "the older and honoured chiefs in natural science" see nothing in your facts to sustain "evolution in any form." You have no facts that directly and unmistakeably prove evolution. The facts you find may be the remote descendants of the facts you do not find, but we need to be assured of their descent. By-and-by we shall consider the "general reasons" which have led some to "believe in the general principle of evolution." But, first, let me request you to observe that, when you speak of "breaks in the organic chain as incessantly occurring in all parts of the series ... as between the orang and its nearest allies, between the Tarsius and the other Lemuridæ," &c., you are taking for granted, instead of proving, the reality of these breaks. They are breaks if your hypothesis is true, but not otherwise.

Homo. It might help our progress in the argument, my Lord, if Mr. Darwin will tell us whether he will undertake to prove, regarding any animal of the present day, that it is, however slowly, yet unquestionably, progressing towards a higher form. In his work "On the Origin of Species," first edition, page 184, he says, "In North America the black bear was seen by Hearne swimming for hours, with a widely open mouth, thus catching, almost like a whale, insects in the water. Even in so extreme a case, if the supply of insects were constant, and if better adapted competitors did not appear, I can see no difficulty in a race of bears being rendered, by Natural Selection, more and more aquatic in their structure and habits, with larger and larger mouths, till a creature was produced as monstrous as a whale."

Lord C. I never heard of a whale catching insects in the water, nor even of a bear doing so. What sort of insects were they?

Homo. That information, my Lord, Mr. Darwin does not give us. It would manifestly require, however, a prodigious quantity of any kind of insects that we are acquainted with to fatten a bear into a whale. But I want to know if Natural Selection is at present carrying on a process of this kind with any race of animals whatever.

Darwin. Homo ought to have mentioned, my Lord, that the passage he has just read is omitted from the subsequent editions of the work in which it appeared.

Homo. I am aware it is omitted, my Lord, and also that no reason for the omission is given. Mr. Darwin does not say whether he omitted it because he had seen reason to change his mind regarding the power of Natural Selection, or whether it was because some of his fellow naturalists thought the statement so monstrous that they requested its suppression. For one might think that, if Natural Selection could turn black bears into creatures like whales, it might also, especially when aided by the contrivances of human reason, turn pigs into creatures like elephants.

Lord C. Are you not going beyond Mr. Darwin, Homo, in conceiving such an idea?

Homo. I think not, my Lord. A pig is quite as like an elephant as a black bear is like a whale. Indeed, the pig has the advantage. Its habitat is on dry land, like that of the bear. Then, its snout bears a remote resemblance to the trunk of an elephant. Lamarck supposed that the giraffe acquired its long neck by having had originally to seek its food in the overhanging branches of trees. The neck was gradually lengthened by being constantly stretched. Now, my Lord, there might surely be some contrivance by which pigs would have to stretch their snouts to reach their food. If there is no difficulty—and Mr. Darwin sees none—in a race of bears becoming changed by Natural Selection into creatures as "monstrous" as whales, why should there be any difficulty in a race of pigs being changed by Natural Selection, aided by human reason, into creatures as "monstrous" as elephants? Mr. Darwin tells us in the last edition of the work in question, page 89, that "pigs have often been born with a sort of proboscis, like that of the tapir or elephant." Let him, then, procure one of these pigs, and he will have the work half done to his hand.

Lord C. Mr. Darwin has, no doubt, changed his opinion on this point; at all events, it is wisely appointed by the Great Author of nature that men shall not be able to play fantastic tricks with the established order of things. Species may certainly be modified within a certain limited range, but each appears to have its bounds, which it cannot pass. If man were able, by crossing, or by placing animals under new conditions, or in any other way, to produce new kinds, why, the world would be full of all sorts of monsters—of creatures more strange than fancy or imagination has ever pictured. Let me now ask Mr. Darwin whether any fossil remains of the "ape-like progenitors of man," or of the "hairy quadruped" which, he says, is the common ancestor of them all, have been found?

Darwin. My Lord, "with respect to the absence of fossil remains serving to connect man with his ape-like progenitors, no one will lay much stress on this fact who will read Sir Charles Lyell's discussion, in which he shows that, in the vertebrate classes, the discovery of fossil remains has been an extremely slow and fortuitous process.

Nor should it be forgotten that those regions which are the most likely to afford remains connecting man with some extinct ape-like creature have not, as yet, been searched by geologists." (Vol. i. p. 201.)

Lord C. To what regions do you refer as most likely to contain such remains?

Darwin. "It is probable," my Lord, "that Africa was formerly inhabited by extinct apes, closely allied to the gorilla and chimpanzee; and as these two species are now man's nearest allies, it is somewhat more probable that our early progenitors lived on the African continent than elsewhere. But it is useless to speculate on this subject, for an ape nearly as large as a man . . . existed in Europe during the Upper Miocene period; and since so remote a period the earth has certainly undergone many great revolutions, and there has been ample time for migration on the largest scale." (Vol. i. p. 199.)

Lord C. Man's progenitors, then, like this ape, may have been Europeans.

Darwin. What I have said, my Lord, implies that.

Lord C. In which case, Europe ought to contain fossil remains of our supposed progenitors; yet you can point to none that have been found in Europe.

Darwin. The discovery of fossil remains, my Lord, as Sir Charles Lyell says, has always "been an extremely slow and fortuitous process."

Lord C. Am I then to understand that, as yet, no fossil remains of any kind have been found anywhere, which can be produced in proof of your hypothesis—no fossil remains, either of the immediate, or the remote, progenitors of man?

Darwin. In answer to this question, I must refer your Lordship to my quotation from Sir Charles Lyell.

Homo. Pray, ask him, my Lord, if geologists have found

fossil remains which they can prove to be those of the progenitors of *any* race of animals now living on the earth. Have they found fossil remains which they can prove to belong to the progenitors of the eagle, or of the horse, or of the donkey, or the whale—of any creature, in short, from a mouse or a mole up to a man? I am aware, indeed, that fossil remains of animals thought to resemble the horse have been found, but Mr. Darwin might as easily prove that the donkey is descended from the dromedary, as that the horses of the present day are descended from the Hippotherium.

Lord C. And yet some naturalists are of this opinion.

Homo. That, my Lord, may very easily be accounted for.

> 'Tis distance lends enchantment to the view;

—distance, aided by these three most potent auxiliaries, Ignorance, Imagination, and Presumption. Why, my Lord, if these extinct forms were now living around us, naturalists would no more venture to affirm them to be the progenitors of the horse, than they dare tell us that our cats are descended from the Bengal tiger, or our dogs from the African lion; or—to take, perhaps, a more apposite case—that the gorilla is the father race to the gibbon and the chimpanzee. Why is it, my Lord, that naturalists do not come into the light of existing facts, and point out to us some living species that has sprung from some other living species? They know that existing facts would not bear them out. Hence they grope their way, by the aid of fossil bones, millions of ages back into the past; and there, amid its pitchy darkness, they fancy they see the desired transformations taking place. Worms become fishes, and fishes change "insensibly" into fowls! Amphibians produce reptiles, and reptiles become the nurses of quadrupeds! Black bears turn into creatures like whales, and the monster Hippotherium gives birth to the horse! Then comes the crowning marvel of all. Quadrupeds produce monkeys, and from monkeys "Man, the wonder and glory of the universe, proceeds." All this, of course, requires time. But there is no difficulty with them about time. The pendulum of Mr. Darwin's clock swings but once in a century. With men of his type of mind, a thousand ages are but as a moment. They know perfectly well what took place during the "Upper Miocene period," myriads of centuries ago. Our men of science can go back almost a whole eternity, even to the time of the primeval mist, when the foundations of the world were laid, and then return and tell us how it was done! Ugh!! I am sick of them and their assumptions, and am reminded by them of those ancient, but too true words, "Professing themselves to be wise, they became fools."

Lord C. You are waxing rhetorical, Homo. I must remind you that facts and calm reasoning have more weight than rhetoric. Besides, must not periods of enormous length have been necessary to work out the changes in the condition of the earth revealed by geology?

Homo. I do not question that at all, my Lord; but I object to men who call themselves "scientific," in order to find support for a favourite hypothesis, leaving the light of ascertained and indisputable facts, groping their way into darkness, which would be felt by any but themselves, and bringing us back from thence mere fancies of their own, which they require us to accept as truths, and which, if received, must tend to darken and degrade the noble nature God has given us. It is clear, my Lord, from the paintings on Egyptian monuments, and the mummies of sacred animals found in Egyptian tombs, that, for three thousand years at least, there has been no change in certain species. They have retained the same general form, and even the same specific differences, for thirty centuries. And man himself has not changed during that time.

Lord C. But is there not a great difference between three thousand years and three million years?

Homo. My Lord, if you multiply nothing by three millions, or even by three hundred millions, it will be nothing still. If three thousand years have literally done nothing to develop one species into another—and this may be demonstrated to be the fact—three thousand million years would do as little.

Lord C. We must return now to the subject of fossil remains. It is clear, Mr. Darwin, that none have as yet been found anywhere, to which you can refer as proving the truth of your hypothesis.

Homo. My Lord, England, and also the Continent, abound in fossil remains. Our chalk hills are full of them, and so are miles upon miles of the earth's strata all around us. Railway contractors have been cutting through them in every direction for nearly half a century; yet geologists cannot supply Mr. Darwin with a bone, or even a tooth, which can help him to prove his assertions, not only as to man's origin, but as to the origin of any species of creature now living. He asserts that all living species have been produced by Natural Selection from other species. Let him, then, produce fossil remains which he can prove to be those of the progenitors of any species of living animal, if he can.

Lord C. It is vain to ask for that, Homo; it appears it can't be done.

Homo. So it seems, my Lord; and thus, while, according to Mr. Darwin, there has been not only a chain of descent connecting man with this hairy quadruped, but also numerous other chains connecting the various monkey and other tribes, now living, with some common progenitor, not only does Mr. Darwin fail to produce those chains, he cannot produce even a fossil link of one of them. Now, my Lord, I submit that this can be accounted for only on the supposition, either that these chains of descent are entirely imaginary and never existed, or that the creatures composing them were cannibals, and so devoured one another—bones and all.

Lord C. We come, then, to this conclusion, Mr. Darwin; that as to "the ape-like progenitors of man," connecting him with this "hairy quadruped," not only is the chain of descent missing, but all the links of the chain as well. You are unable to produce any one of those links. But further, according to your hypothesis, every distinct species of animal now existing is descended from the same primary stock with man. There must, therefore, have been "a series of forms graduating insensibly" from the primary creature, whatever it was, to each distinct kind of animal now existing. In short, there must have been chains of descent as numerous as present living species. If you could produce some of these chains of descent, or even one of them, it would go so far towards rendering it probable that man, also, has his chain of descent, though, unfortunately, every link of it is missing. But, as in the case of man, so in the case of all other species—you cannot show the chain of descent of one of them, or produce fossil evidence that it ever existed.

Darwin. As I have already remarked, my Lord, "no one will lay much stress on this fact, who will read Sir Charles Lyell's discussion."

SECOND DAY'S SITTING.

Lord C. We come now, Mr. Darwin, to the "general reasons" which you regard as proving "the general principle of evolution." Will you begin the statement of them?

Darwin. First, my Lord, "there is *the Bodily Structure of Man.* It is notorious that man is constructed on the same general type or model with other mammals. All the bones in his skeleton can be compared with corresponding bones in a monkey, bat, or seal. So it is with his muscles, nerves, blood-vessels, and internal viscera. The brain, the most important of all the organs, follows the same law, as shown by Huxley and other anatomists." (Vol. i. p. 10.)

Homo. I freely admit, my Lord, the general correctness of the statement Mr. Darwin has just made. There can be no question as to man possessing an animal nature. Who doubts it? The belief of this is, I suppose, as ancient as man himself. Neither can there be any question as to man's bodily frame being constructed on the same general type as that of other mammals. How could it be otherwise? Like other mammals, man is made to live, and move, and have his being on the earth. He eats and drinks like them. He has numerous functions to perform, precisely similar to theirs. Hence, necessarily, his bodily structure is similar. I do not see how he could have been constructed otherwise. Perhaps Mr. Darwin can suggest some better type after which man's physical nature might have been modelled.

Darwin. That is a task, my Lord, which I have not attempted.

Homo. And very wisely so, my Lord. He could as little have succeeded in it, as in producing a new species from an old one, or in finding the missing links of some one of the missing chains. Every animal is adapted by its structure for its habitat and mode of life. Creatures of the ape kind, for example, with a rude kind of hands, and feet which are also hands, being fitted for clutching branches and climbing trees, are essentially arboreal in their habits. They never willingly leave the forest, where they find at once suitable food and needful security. Mr. Darwin would as little succeed in showing, in the case of an ape, as in the case of a man, that it might have been more suitably modelled than it is. If he asks me why my bodily structure somewhat resembles that of an ape, I reply—Certainly not because I am descended from an ape, but because I require, for my habitat and mode of life, precisely such a bodily structure as I possess. Mr. Darwin should show that man's bodily structure might have been better modelled before he argues from it that I am descended from an ape. If this argument, in itself, be worth anything, it would prove, quite as conclusively, that the ape is descended from man.

Lord C. If you could show, Mr. Darwin, that man's bodily structure is an inconvenience to him, or that it might have been more suitably modelled, this would go so far towards supporting your argument. On the supposition of man having been separately created, we can imagine the Creator moulding his animal nature after the same general type as that of other mammals, though we can hardly suppose Him following that type so far as thereby to subject this new and superior creature to disadvantage. It appears to me an important point that man's bodily structure should be so wonderfully—so perfectly adapted to the purposes for which man requires it. On your hypothesis, man owes it entirely to the power of Natural Selection that he is what he is!

Homo. Mr. Darwin, my Lord, endows what he calls Natural Selection, with all that power and wisdom which we are accustomed to attribute to the Almighty. In his work on "The Origin of Species," he says regarding it, "It may be metaphorically said that Natural Selection is daily and hourly scrutinizing, throughout the world, the slightest variations; rejecting those that are bad, preserving and adding up all that are good; silently and insensibly working, whenever and wherever opportunity offers, at the improvement of each organic being in relation to its organic and inorganic conditions of life." (p. 96.)

Darwin. My Lord, "the time will, before long, come when it will be thought wonderful that naturalists, who were well acquainted with the comparative structure and development of man and other mammals, should have believed that each was the work of a separate act of creation." (Vol. i. p. 33.)

Lord C. That, at all events, is, at present, the prevailing belief of man himself as to his origin.

Darwin. "In my work," my Lord, "on 'THE ORIGIN OF SPECIES,' I had two distinct objects in view : firstly, to show that species had not been separately created ; and secondly, that Natural Selection had been the chief agent of change;" . . . and if, in that work, " I have erred in giving to Natural Selection great powers, which I am far from admitting, or in having exaggerated its power, which is in itself probable, I have, at least, as I hope, done good service in aiding to overthrow the dogma of separate creations." (Vol. i. pp. 152, 153.)

Lord C. You should not allow your feeling against this "dogma," as you call it, to influence you too strongly. If you can show it to be a mere dogma, by establishing your own belief on a basis of ascertained and indisputable facts, it will soon wither and perish. But, as we have seen, you are at present building your hypothesis, not on facts, but on "general reasons."

Homo. My Lord, what is Mr. Darwin's hypothesis but a dogma? It is Darwin's dogma of man's development by Natural Selection, against the Bible doctrine of man's creation by the power of the Almighty.

Darwin. I should also mention, my Lord, that "man is liable to receive from the lower animals, and to communicate to them, certain diseases, as hydrophobia, variola, the glanders, &c.; and this fact proves the close similarity of their tissues and blood, both in minute structure and composition, far more plainly than does their comparison under the best microscope, or by the aid of the best chemical analysis. Monkeys are liable to many of the same non-contagious diseases as we are . . . to catarrh . . . apoplexy, inflammation of the bowels, and cataract in the eyes . . . Medicines produce the same effect on them as on us. Many kinds of monkeys have a strong taste for tea, coffee, and spirituous liquors; they will also, as I have myself seen, smoke tobacco with pleasure . . . These trifling facts show how similar the nerves of taste must be in monkeys and man, and how similarly their whole nervous system is affected." (Vol. i. pp. 11, 12.)

Lord C. No one, I presume, will dispute the facts you now state; but similarity of nervous system in man and monkey, and liability to some of the same diseases, is one thing, their community of descent is quite another. I have a horse that catches cold occasionally; he has also a strong relish for gooseberries; he will follow me all over the field, drawn by the attraction of a ripe apple; but it never occurred to me to infer from these facts that my horse is sprung from the same progenitors with myself.

Homo. My Lord, the world has been familiar with such facts for thousands of years. We must suppose, therefore, I presume, that it has been man's " prejudice and natural arrogance" that have hitherto prevented him from drawing from them the conclusion which Mr. Darwin now draws for him.

Darwin. The next line of proof to which I shall direct your Lordship's attention is that of "*Embryonic Development.* Man is developed from an ovule about the 125th of an inch in diameter, which differs in no respect from the ovules of other animals. The embryo itself, at a very early period, can hardly be distinguished from that of other members of the vertebrate kingdom." (Vol. i. p. 14.)

Lord C. Am to understand you as affirming that the ovule from which man is developed " differs *in no respect* from the ovules of other animals"?

Darwin. That is precisely what I do affirm, my Lord.

Lord C. It seems to me, then, I must say, that your statement is most incautious. If you had said that the human ovule differs in no respect *that you can discern* from that of other animals, I should not have objected to it. But it is clear that, in objects so minute, there may be differences, though you are unable to detect them. Indeed, as it appears to me, there must be an essential difference, for it is unquestionable that the ovule of a dog can produce but a dog, while the human ovule produces man. I cannot see, then, what ground you have for affirming that the human ovule " differs *in no respect* from the ovules of other animals."

Homo. If Mr. Darwin believes, my Lord, that the ovules

of animals "differ in no respect" from one another, then he must also believe that it is only because of the different conditions under which they are developed, that different creatures are produced from them. Under the same conditions the result would be the same, and all born creatures might be donkeys, monkeys, or men. It follows, also, that in the germ, all creatures are not only similar, but absolutely identical. Originally, there is no difference between a man and a rhinoceros, or between a chimpanzee and a sheep.

Lord C. Mr. Darwin will doubtless think of this, and will, perhaps, modify his language in subsequent editions of his work.

Darwin. My Lord, "as some readers of my book may never have seen a drawing of an embryo, I have given one of man, and another of a dog, at about the same early stage of development, carefully copied from two works of undoubted accuracy." (Vol. i. pp. 14, 15.)

Lord C. (*Examining the drawing.*) The difference is certainly quite as striking as the resemblance. Any intelligent child could indicate the points of dissimilarity.

Homo. And yet, my Lord, the ovules from which such developments proceed, "differ in no respect" from one another.

Darwin. My Lord, "it would be superfluous on my part to give a number of borrowed details, showing that the embryo of man closely resembles that of other mammals. It may, however, be added, that the human embryo likewise resembles, in various points of structure, certain low forms when adult." (Vol. i. p. 16).

Lord C. I suppose that no one who has looked into the matter will deny that, in the germs and embryonic beginnings of all vertebrate creatures, there are points of

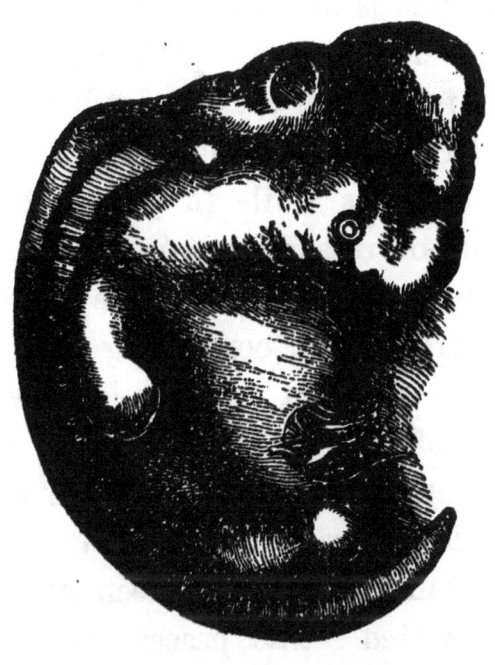

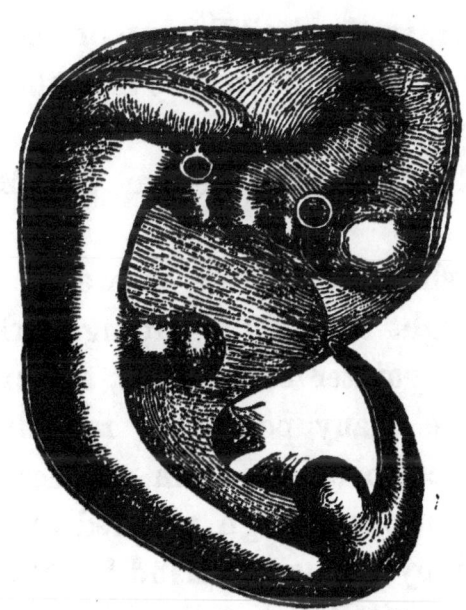

Upper figure, a human embryo, much magnified, after Ecker. Lower figure, embryo of a dog, also magnified, after Bischoff.—Copied from Mr. Darwin's work on "The Descent of Man."

resemblance. This is not strange considering what we all admit, viz., that man is constructed on the same general type or model with other mammals. If there are points of resemblance between full-grown men and full-grown animals, it would be singular indeed were there no points of resemblance between their embryos while in process of development. But these points of resemblance in their embryos do not prove them to be sprung from the same progenitors.

Homo. My Lord, I was conversing on this subject the other day with a gentleman who has long been engaged in the manufacture of steam engines. Every one that he has produced has been constructed on the same general type. Each of them has a general resemblance to the others. And this resemblance might have been detected while they were being fabricated. The process of manufacture was similar in the case of all of them. Why, then, may not the All-wise Creator, in the building up of the material framework of the successive creatures He has called into existence, pursue a similar course?

Lord C. That is a question for Mr. Darwin to answer.

Homo. But which he has not answered, my Lord. The same remark might be made regarding works of art. The productions of a painter or sculptor, for example, in their beginnings have many points of resemblance; but are they therefore developed one from another? Are they not all separate creations, though planned by the same mind, and elaborated by the same hand? And does not the painter or sculptor try that each of his productions should advance on those that have preceded it? Does he not also bring forward, as far as he can, into each successive production, all the knowledge, and skill, and power, that have distinguished his former productions? It seems to me my Lord, that, in the physical structure of man, and in the building up of that structure, we see just a similar principle at work. Mr. Darwin might as well maintain that all steam engines have been developed from the tea-kettle, or all paintings or sculptures from some common prototype, as that man, because of some points of resemblance in his structure and development to those of the lower animals, is sprung from the same stock with them.

Darwin. You know, my Lord, how I feel regarding that dogma of "separate acts of creation," on which Homo seems now to be falling back.

Lord C. I am well aware how you feel regarding it, Mr. Darwin, but, as you see, Homo also has his feelings. He evidently prefers believing that man has been created immediately by the Divine Being, to believing that he is descended from " a hairy quadruped, with a tail and pointed ears," and more remotely from a worm. He thinks, too, that he has good grounds for his belief. What is the next point?

Darwin. "*Rudiments*," my Lord. "Rudimentary organs . . . are either absolutely useless, such as the mammæ of male quadrupeds, or the incisor teeth of ruminants which never cut through the gums; or they are of such slight service to their present possessors that we cannot suppose that they were developed under the conditions which now exist . . . Rudimentary organs are eminently variable. . . . They often become wholly suppressed. When this occurs they are nevertheless liable to occasional reappearance through reversion. . . . Every one must have noticed the power which many animals, especially horses, possess of moving or twitching their skin; and this is effected by the panniculus carnosus. Remnants of this muscle, in an efficient state, are found in various parts of our bodies;

D

for instance, on the forehead, by which the eyebrows are raised . . Some few persons have the power of contracting the superficial muscles on their scalps, and these muscles are in a variable and partially rudimentary condition. M. A. de Candolle has communicated to me a curious instance of the long continued persistence or inheritance of this power, as well as of its unusual development. He knows a family in which one member, the present head of a family, could, when a youth, pitch several heavy books from his head by the movement of the scalp alone; and he won wagers by performing this feat." (Vol. i. pp. 17-20.)

Homo. I question, my Lord, whether Mr. Darwin could produce any one of the lower animals capable of performing this feat. I know there are horses that can win wagers by racing, but I never yet heard of one that could do so by pitching heavy books from his head by the movement of the scalp alone. No animal can do this. It is idle therefore to refer to the case Mr. Darwin has adduced, as an instance of rudimentary structure. As to man's power of raising his eyebrows and wrinkling his forehead, it is part of the "power of face" with which his Maker has endued him. But there is a great difference between a horse twitching his skin, when tickled or stung by a fly, and a naturalist raising his eyebrows when he thinks he has detected some fresh rudimentary structure in man which will justify his classing him with the lower animals. Perhaps Mr. Darwin will tell us how it happens that a man can express high intelligence, deep thought, loving sympathy, by the movements of the muscles of his face alone, while a horse cannot express them by twitching his skin all his body over.

Darwin. My Lord, "Professor Turner, of Edinburgh, has informed me that he has occasionally detected muscular fasciculi in five different situations, namely, in the axillæ, near the scapulæ, &c., all of which must be referred to the system of the panniculus." (Vol. i. p. 19.)

Lord C. You have just said that "rudimentary organs are eminently variable." Is it not also so with the muscles of the human body? Do they not vary in different individuals?

Darwin. "The muscles" of the human body "are eminently variable," my Lord. "Thus, those of the foot were found by Professor Turner not to be strictly alike in any two out of fifty bodies... Mr. J. Wood has recorded the occurrence of 295 muscular variations in thirty-six subjects, and in another set of the same number, no less than 558 variations, reckoning both sides of the body as one.... A single body presented the extraordinary number of twenty-five distinct abnormalities.... The famous old anatomist, Wolff, insists that the internal viscera are more variable than the external parts.... He has even written a treatise on the choice of typical examples of the viscera for representation." (Vol. i. p. 109.)

Lord C. I presume that, as to his physical structure, man varies as much internally as he does externally?

Darwin. "It is manifest," my Lord, "that man is now subject to much variability. No two individuals of the same race are quite alike. We may compare millions of faces, and each will be distinct. There is an equally great amount of diversity in the proportions and dimensions of the various parts of the body; the length of the legs being one of the most variable points." (Vol. i. p. 108.)

Lord C. How do you think those variations are to be accounted for?

Darwin. "With respect to the causes of variability," my Lord, "we are in all cases very ignorant; but we can see that in man, as in the lower animals, they stand in some relation with the conditions to which each species has been exposed during several generations. Domesticated animals vary more than those in a state of nature; and this is apparently due to the diversified and changing nature of their conditions. The different races of man resemble in this respect domesticated animals. . . . We see the influence of diversified conditions in the more civilized nations. . . . The uniformity of savages has often been exaggerated, and, in some cases can hardly be said to exist." (Vol. i. p. 141.)

Lord C. No one can doubt the existence of numerous variations in man and the lower animals, but we need not at present inquire further into its causes. Doubtless, as you say, "we are in all cases very ignorant" as "to the causes of variability." The point now to be considered is— Does the existence of such variations, as you have just told us Professor Turner, of Edinburgh, has informed you of, prove man to be allied to the lower animals? Do they show him to be descended from the "hairy quadruped" you speak of, or from the larvæ of ancient Ascidians?

Darwin. "In order," my Lord, "that an ape-like creature should have been transformed into man, it is necessary that this early form, as well as many successive links, should all have varied in mind and body. It is impossible to obtain direct evidence on this head; but if it can be shown that man now varies—that his variations are induced by the same general causes, and by the same general laws, as in the case of the lower animals—there can be little doubt that the preceding intermediate links varied in a like manner." (Vol. i. p. 107.)

Lord C. I should say there can be no doubt whatever that if "the preceding intermediate links" ever really existed, they "varied" just as men and animals vary now. But you have first to prove that they really have existed.

The fact that man now varies shows that he has got an animal nature, but I cannot, for the life of me, see how this circumstance proves him to be connected with the lower animals in descent. On the supposition that man exists as the result of a separate act of creation, it might be expected that, exposed as he is to so many diversified and changing conditions, his bodily structure would exhibit, both internally and externally, quite as numerous variations as are found in it.

Homo. My Lord, Mr. Darwin, after stating what he calls "the laws of variation," tells us that they apply, "most of them, even to plants." (Vol. i. p. 113). Now, we know that plants of the same kind vary among themselves endlessly. The oak, for example, varies both in its roots below and in its branches above. I suppose that, as in man, "the length of the legs is one of the most variable points," so in the oak is the length of its roots and branches. Will Mr. Darwin maintain, then, that the variations in an oak tree, and among them the different lengths of its roots and branches, prove the oak to be descended from some lower vegetable form?

Darwin. My Lord, allow me to remind you that my argument, derived from rudimentary muscles connected with the panniculus, referred to by Professor Turner, has not been answered.

Lord C. What has Homo to say in reply to it?

Homo. I would say first, my Lord, in Mr. Darwin's own words, that "with respect to the causes of variability we are in all cases very ignorant;" and secondly, that as "the muscles are eminently variable," and as "a single body presented the extraordinary number of twenty-five distinct abnormalities," it should hardly surprise us that these "variations" and "abnormalities" sometimes take the direction pointed out by Professor Turner. I may also remind your Lordship of the gentleman Mr. Darwin told us of, who "could pitch several heavy books from his head by the movement of the scalp alone." No horse has got muscles connected with the panniculus which could enable him to perform this feat; nor has any other animal that I ever heard of. Perhaps, however, Mr. Darwin may think that some animal, now extinct, possessed this extraordinary power.

Lord C. We had better confine our attention to what Mr. Darwin says. We need not take what he may think into account. Will he now go on?

Darwin. My Lord, "the extrinsic muscles which serve to move the whole external ear, and the intrinsic muscles which move the different parts, all of which belong to the system of the panniculus, are in a rudimentary condition in man; they are also variable in development, or at least in function. I have seen one man who could draw his ears forwards, and another who could draw them backwards, and from what one of these persons told me it is probable that most of us, by often touching our ears, and thus directing attention to them, could, by repeated trials, recover some power of movement. The faculty of erecting the ears, and of directing them to different points of the compass, is, no doubt, of the highest service to many animals, as they thus perceive the point of danger; but I have never heard of a man who possessed the least power of erecting his ears— the one movement which might be of use to him. . . . The ears of the chimpanzee and orang are curiously like those of man, and I am assured by the keepers in the Zoological Gardens that these animals never move or erect them; so that they are in an equally rudimentary condition, as far as function is concerned, as in man. Why these animals, as well as the progenitors of man, should have lost the power of erecting their ears, we cannot say. It may be, though I am not quite satisfied with this view, that, owing to their arboreal habits and great strength, they were but little exposed to danger, and so, during a lengthened period, moved their ears but little, and thus gradually lost the power of moving them." (Vol. i. pp. 20-22.)

Homo. You were asking Mr. Darwin, a little while ago, my Lord, whether man suffers any inconvenience from his bodily structure being modelled like that of an ape. It now appears that he does; he has lost the power of "erecting his ears, the one movement which might be of use to him!" Why should he not try, " by often touching his ears, and directing his attention to them," to recover this lost power? Our national schoolmasters might occasionally exercise their pupils in this direction. " Erect your ears, boys," might come in as part of the daily drill. If this faculty, which Mr. Darwin tells us we have lost, could be recovered, and man were able, like a donkey, or a horse, to direct his ears to different points of the compass, he would so far have the advantage over his relations in the Zoological Gardens.

Lord C. The schoolmaster had better leave this matter to Mr. Darwin and the younger naturalists. As to the power of erecting his ears being a faculty that would be of use to man, I should think he possesses a more useful faculty in being able easily to turn his head in any direction he pleases. When you say, Mr. Darwin, that you cannot tell " why the progenitors of man should have lost the power of erecting their ears," are you not taking for granted what should first be proved, viz., that man has had progenitors which possessed the power in question?

Homo. Perhaps, my Lord, Mr. Darwin will tell us how man's supposed progenitors came to have external ears at all. I should like him to trace the development of the external ear from the Ascidian to the ape, or at least to explain the process to us, and show some proof that his account of it is anything more than a mere product of his imagination. As to the whole external shell of the ear being a rudiment, and therefore useless, I should like to know how man would look without it ; yet, if Mr. Darwin's principles be true, we must, I suppose, eventually lose our ears, just as we have lost our tails !

Lord C. That does not follow, Homo. Mr. Darwin's principle of "Sexual Selection" would, I presume, come into play here. Ladies would certainly object to a husband with a tail ; hence the tail must go : but as they would hardly choose one without ears, the ears, I suppose, must remain.

Homo. And thus, my Lord, the fact of man having retained his ears while losing his tail would be accounted for.

Lord C. At all events, Mr. Darwin, quite apart from the question of rudiments, humanity would certainly object to losing its ears.

Darwin. My Lord, "the celebrated sculptor, Mr. Woolner, informs me of one little peculiarity in the external ear, which he has often observed both in men and women, and of which he perceived the full signification. . . . The peculiarity consists in a little blunt point, projecting from the inwardly folded margin or helix. Mr. Woolner made an exact model of one such case, and has sent me the accompanying drawing. These points not only project inwards, but often a little outwards, so that they are visible when the head is viewed from directly in front or behind. They are variable in size and somewhat in position, standing either a little higher or lower, and they sometimes occur on one ear and not on the other. Now the meaning of these projections is not, I think, doubtful. . . . The helix obviously consists of the extreme margin of the ear folded inwards; and this folding appears to be in some manner connected with the whole external ear being permanently pressed backwards. In many monkeys, which do not stand high in the order, as baboons and some species of macacus, the upper portion of the ear is slightly pointed, and the margin is not at all folded inwards; but if the margin were to be thus folded, a slight point would necessarily project inwards, and probably a little outwards. This could actually be observed in a specimen of the *Ateles Beelzebuth* in the Zoological Gardens; and we may safely conclude that it is a similar structure—a vestige of formerly pointed ears—which occasionally re-appears in man." (Vol. i. pp. 22, 23.)

Lord C. The ladies will not thank you, Mr. Darwin, for finding "the Mark of the Beast" on so prominent a bodily member. Those of them who, unfortunately, have it, will now be covering it over from observation. We have heard a good deal of late about M.B. coats; we shall be hearing next, I suppose, of M.B. ears. But how do you account, Homo, for those points to which Mr. Darwin directs attention, as occasionally appearing on the ear?

Homo. Why should not the ear, my Lord, like other portions of man's structure, be modelled after preceding types? The figure of this organ, drawn by Mr. Woolner, looks reputable enough, even though it may have a point. Mr. Darwin has told us that the famous old anatomist, Wolff, wrote " a treatise on the choice of typical examples of the viscera." Perhaps some rising naturalist may favour us, some day, with a treatise on typical examples of the ear. As to this point appearing only occasionally, I can no more account for it than I can account for other variations which appear only occasionally. If, in no two persons is the shape of the ear exactly alike, neither is the colour of the eye. Some persons have black eyes, some have blue eyes, and some have them grey, or even green; but I don't suppose that the fact of some of the lower animals having eyes similarly coloured would prove them to be our relations. Mr. Darwin speaks of "the whole external ear being permanently pressed backwards," but he does not tell us how, or by whom, this was done.

Lord C. Is not that portion of the ear called the lobe, occasionally wanting? I have seen persons with scarcely any lobe whatever to their ears. Would Mr. Darwin argue from this fact that the hairy quadruped—man's progenitor —while he had pointed ears, was unprovided with the appendage to which ladies are so fond of attaching ornaments?

Homo. Mr. Darwin, my Lord, will perhaps reply to that question in some subsequent edition of his work. But I beg to suggest another point for his consideration. It is well known that the nose varies in development, as well as the ear, and that, occasionally, persons have what is called the aquiline nose. Are we to regard this as a vestige of a formerly aquiline nose possessed by our ape-like progenitors,

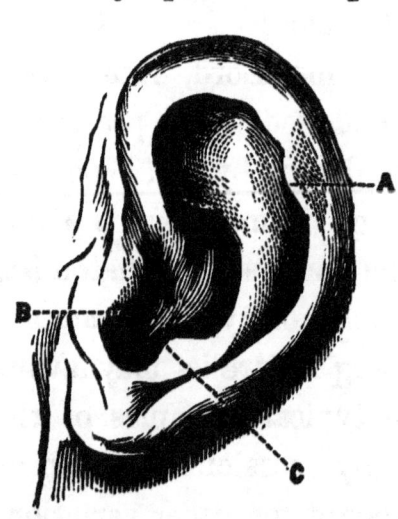

or as an indication that we are allied to the eagle and the parrot, the beaks of these creatures, and even the mandibles of the cuttle-fish, often having this peculiar curve? I beg also to remark that there are other points on the ear besides the one in question, which Mr. Woolner does not show on his model, and to which Mr. Darwin does not refer. In this engraving, Mr. Woolner's point is shown at A, the other points at B and C.

Lord C. Natural Selection would thus seem to be rather fond of developing points on the ear. But those additional points to which you direct attention, are probably of some use to us.

Homo. Your Lordship forgets that Mr. Darwin considers the whole external shell of the ear to be a rudiment, and therefore useless.

Darwin. My Lord, "the nictitating membrane, or third eyelid, with its accessory muscles and other structures, is especially well developed in birds, and is of much functional importance to them, as it can be rapidly drawn across the whole eyeball. It is found in some reptiles, and amphibians, and in certain fishes, as in sharks. It is fairly well developed in the two lower divisions of the mammalian series, namely, in the Monotremata and Marsupials, and in some few of the higher mammals, as in the walrus. But in man, the quadrumana, and most other mammals, it exists, as is admitted by all anatomists, as a mere rudiment, called the semilunar fold." (Vol. i. p. 23.)

Homo. As with man's ears, my Lord, so with his eyes. Why should they not be modelled after the type of preceding forms? Mr. Darwin tells us that this membrane is of "much functional importance to birds, as it can be rapidly drawn across the whole eyeball." But this is only like telling us that the eye is of much functional importance to them, as they can see with it; or the wing, as they can fly with it; or the stomach, as they can digest their food with it. Mr. Darwin should rather have told us how it comes to pass on the principle of Natural Selection, that while birds and sharks and kangaroos have this membrane, men and monkeys should be destitute of it. Their having the semilunar fold can easily be accounted for by the doctrine of typical forms; but I do not see how Natural Selection can have robbed them of the third eyelid, supposing they had ancient progenitors who possessed it.

Lord C. No doubt, Mr. Darwin, by the exercise of a little ingenuity, could give some explanation of this point.

Homo. Imagination, my Lord, is a great power with Mr. Darwin, but very probably he would say—"With respect to the causes (of the loss of the third eyelid by the mammalia) we are in all cases very ignorant."

Darwin. "The sense of smell," my Lord, "is of the highest importance to the greater number of mammals—to some, as the ruminants, in warning them of danger; to others, as the carnivora, in finding their prey; to others, as the wild boar, for both purposes combined. But the sense of smell is of extremely slight service, if any, even to savages, in whom it is generally more highly developed than in the civilized races. It does not warn them of danger, nor guide them to their food; nor does it prevent the Esquimaux from sleeping in the most fœtid atmosphere, nor many savages from eating half-putrid meat. Those who believe in the principle of gradual evolution will not readily admit that this sense, in its present state, was originally acquired by man, as he now exists. No doubt he inherits the power in an enfeebled, and so far rudimentary condition, from some early progenitor, to whom it was highly serviceable, and by whom it was continually used. We can thus, perhaps, understand how it is, as Dr. Maudsley has truly remarked, that the sense of smell in man 'is singularly effective in recalling vividly the ideas and images of forgotten scenes and places;' for we see in those animals which have this sense highly developed, such as dogs and horses, that old recollections of persons and places are strongly associated with their odour." (Vol. i. pp. 23, 24.)

Homo. How can Mr. Darwin say, my Lord, that our sense of smell is of "extremely slight service" to us, or that we have it in a "rudimentary condition"? The odours wafted from the flowers in his own garden might have taught him otherwise. We should be in constant danger of being blown up by gas, or poisoned by the effluvium from sewers, were it not for our having this sense. But I forgot that Mr. Darwin believes that our forefathers were savages, and that there were neither gardens, gas, nor sewers in their days.

Lord C. I am surprised, Mr. Darwin, at what you say regarding the sense of smell. If it does not assist us, as it does the carnivora, in finding our prey, it certainly warns us of danger, and is often a source of enjoyment. But if it were more fully developed than it is, it might often be a cause of annoyance to us. One would not like, for example, to be always smelling a rat, even when rats are near; or to be reminded, by certain odours, of places and persons we would rather forget.

Homo. My Lord, Mr. Darwin may not find this sense of much use to himself, but he will find few among his human allies of his opinion regarding it. Will you observe, my Lord, how constantly Mr. Darwin recurs to *savage* life in illustrating his subject? He seems to forget that he is a member of civilized society, and has to do with civilized men.

Lord C. You must remember, Homo, what you have just said. "Mr. Darwin believes that our forefathers were savages;" he argues therefore on this supposition.

Homo. I know he does, my Lord; but, according to him Natural Selection, which has done such wonders in developing man's intellect and perfecting his bodily structure, has made a great mistake with the sense of smell. It is "of extremely slight service," he tells us, "even to savages." As to ourselves, he seems to regard it as of use to us only in helping memory. Natural Selection has thus dealt unwisely with us, according to Mr. Darwin, as regards the sense of smell. Now, I think, my Lord, that this opinion of his arises from his contemplating man too exclusively from a *savage* point of view. Those who believe that man was not originally a savage, and that he was created with physical powers much the same as he possesses now, can find no fault with the development in him of the sense in question.

Lord C. You mean that what Mr. Darwin says regarding the sense of smell in man, seems to indicate that he thinks himself wiser than Natural Selection.

Homo. Precisely so, my Lord. He evidently thinks that, had he been counsellor, he could have taught Natural Selection better. He would have advised that man should not inherit this sense in so "enfeebled, and so far rudimentary a condition" as that in which he possesses it.

Lord C. In this case, then, I think Mr. Darwin's counsel would not have been good. But what is the next point that comes before us?

Darwin. "There can be little doubt," my Lord, "that the hairs scattered over the body" of man "are the rudiments of the uniform hairy coat of the lower animals." (Vol. i. pp. 24, 25).

Homo. I think there is great doubt of this, my Lord; but perhaps Mr. Darwin will now tell us how it happens that man has lost the hairy coat of his progenitors?

Darwin. I shall willingly do so, my Lord. A "most conspicuous difference between man and the lower animals is the nakedness of his skin. Whales and dolphins (Cetacea), dugongs (Sirenia), and the hippopotamus are naked, and this may be of advantage to them in gliding through the water; nor would it be injurious to them from the loss of warmth, as the species which inhabit the colder regions are protected by a thick layer of blubber, serving the same purpose as the fur of seals and otters. Elephants and rhinoceroses are almost hairless; and as certain extinct species which formerly lived under an arctic climate were covered with long wool or hair, it would almost appear as if the existing species of both genera had lost their hairy covering from exposure to heat. This appears the more probable, as the elephants in India which live in cool and elevated districts are more hairy than those in the lowlands. May we then infer that man became divested of hair from having aboriginally inhabited some tropical land ? (Vol. i. pp. 148, 149.)

Homo. That question is very modestly put, my Lord; but how about the hair of the head?

Darwin. I was going to remark, my Lord, that "the crown of the head" in man "offers a curious exception, for at all times it must have been one of the most exposed parts, yet it is thickly clothed with hair. In this respect, man agrees with the great majority of quadrupeds, which generally have their upper and exposed surfaces more thickly clothed than the lower surface. Nevertheless, my Lord, the fact that all the other members of the order of Primates,* to which man belongs, although inhabiting various hot regions, are well clothed with hair, generally thickest on the upper surface, is strongly opposed

---

* The Primates, according to Linnæus, include man, mon ey, lemur, and bat.

to the supposition that man became naked through the action of the sun." (Vol. i. p. 149.)

Lord C. That is a very candid admission, Mr. Darwin.

Homo. Doubtless it is, my Lord; and also a very wise admission, the thing being almost self-evident. But will Mr. Darwin now tell us how man lost his hairy covering?

Darwin. "I am inclined to believe," my Lord, "as we shall see under Sexual Selection, that man, or rather, primarily woman, became divested of hair for ornamental purposes; and according to this belief, it is not surprising that man should differ so greatly in hairiness from all his lower brethren, for characters gained through Sexual Selection often differ, in closely related forms, to an extraordinary degree." (Vol. i. pp. 149, 150.)

Homo. A most extraordinary supposition, my Lord! Man was originally a hairy animal himself, and hence other hairy animals were his "brethren." Probably, in those days, the whale, and the dolphin, and the hippopotamus, had not become so hairless as they are now. It seems somewhat singular, then, that female whales, female elephants, female rhinoceroses, and female savages, should all of them have become possessed of the desire to get rid of their hairy coverings; that they should have induced the same desire in the other sex; and that, in obedience to this desire, the hair on the bodies of all should have become "small by degrees, and beautifully less"!

Darwin. I did not say, my Lord, that whales were ever covered with hair.

Homo. I beg Mr. Darwin's pardon, my Lord, but I supposed that, belonging as they do to the mammalia, whales might, in former times, have been hairy, like their "brethren" of that order; but I do not insist on this even though, as I believe, whales retain a few bristles about the mouth.

Darwin. Neither did I say, my Lord, that the elephant and hippopotamus "had become divested of hair for ornamental purposes." I said, "It would almost appear as if they had lost their hairy covering from exposure to heat."

Homo. Very true, my Lord, he said so; but he seems not quite sure about its being true.

Lord C. Neither is he as to the way in which man ceased to be hairy. He merely says he is "inclined to believe" it happened in the way he states.

Homo. Then, my Lord, it is altogether supposition. But, granting for the moment that we had such savage maternal progenitors as Mr. Darwin catches an obscure glimpse of, in the dim and far distant past, I question whether they would have wished to lose their hairy covering. Ladies clothe themselves with the furs of animals now. The skin of fine-looking wild beasts is prized by them for its beauty, and used for ornamental purposes. There were neither silks, nor satins, nor coloured prints in those primitive times. It seems to me, therefore, that, if the matter had depended on the savage ladies of those days, the human race would have been hairy still.

Lord C. Mr. Darwin would find it difficult to account for the beauty of the vegetable world on the principles of either Natural or Sexual Selection.

Homo. Or of both of them combined, my Lord.

Darwin. Nevertheless, my Lord, "the early progenitors of man were no doubt once covered with hair, both sexes having beards." (Vol. i. p. 206.)

THIRD DAY'S SITTING.

Lord C. What is the next point?

Darwin. "I am informed by Mr. Paget," my Lord, "that persons belonging to the same family often have a few hairs in their eyebrows much longer than the others, so that this slight peculiarity seems to be inherited. These hairs apparently represent the vibrissæ, which are used as organs of touch by many of the lower animals." (Vol. i. p. 25.)

Lord C. That seems a rather far-fetched inference, Mr. Darwin. Some animals have long hairs about the mouth and face—as, for example, rats and cats—which they use as feelers, and which they certainly inherit. Some men have occasionally long hairs projecting from the eyebrows, which they do *not* use as feelers, and which they *seem* to inherit. We should, therefore, you argue, regard animals possessing these vibrissæ, as co-descendants with us from some ancient progenitor! Your premises certainly do not seem to conduct to your conclusion.

Homo. Perhaps, my Lord—as Mr. Darwin remarked regarding the power of erecting the ear—those persons who have these long hairs projecting from their eyebrows, "by often touching them, and directing attention towards them, could by repeated trials recover some power in them," and so be able to use them as feelers. This would be a good fact for Mr. Darwin, if he could find it so. He would not then have to say, "these hairs *apparent'y* represent the vibrissæ." It is clear he is not quite certain on this point.

Lord C. Why, then, does he put it forward as evidence?

Homo. A drowning man, my Lord, will catch at a straw, or even at a hair, if he can find one to catch at.

Darwin. "In a young chimpanzee," my Lord, "I observed that a few upright, rather long hairs projected above the eyes, where the true eyebrows, if present, would have stood." (Vol. i. p. 25.)

Homo. I do not see, my Lord, that this fact helps Mr. Darwin in the least. Nor does the farther fact—on which, however, he makes no comment—that man possesses eyebrows at all. He has told us "rudimentary organs" are "either absolutely useless," or of very "slight service to their present possessors." Now, our eyebrows, while contributing much to the comeliness and beauty of the human frame, are certainly of no use to us whatever. We could get on very well without them. How came we then to possess them? On the principle of Natural Selection, we ought to have been destitute of these hairy appendages to the brow.

Lord C. Perhaps Sexual Selection will account for the eyebrows.

Homo. That is very questionable, my Lord. Some savage tribes eradicate their eyebrows, and, according to Mr. Darwin, man was originally a savage.

Darwin. My Lord, "the fine wool-like hair, or so-called lanugo, with which the human fœtus, during the sixth month, is thickly covered, offers a more curious case. It is first developed during the fifth month on the eyebrows and face, and especially round the mouth, where it is much longer than that on the head. . . . . The whole surface, including even the forehead and ears, is thus thickly clothed; but it is a significant fact that the palms of the hands and the soles of the feet are quite naked, like the inferior surfaces of all four extremities in most of the lower animals. As this can hardly be an accidental coincidence, we must consider the woolly covering of the fœtus to be the rudimental representation of the first permanent coat of hair in those mammals which are born hairy." (Vol. i. pp. 25, 26.)

Homo. I suppose, my Lord, that the palms of our hands and the soles of our feet—like the inferior surfaces of all four extremities in most of the lower animals—being designed for walking or working, were not intended to be covered with hair, as, in fact, they never are. But how the circumstance of our resembling the lower animals in this respect, can prove the woolly covering of the human embryo to be the rudimental representative of the first permanent hairy coat of the hairy mammals, I cannot comprehend.

Lord C. But how do you account, Homo, for this fine wool-like hair, which covers you before birth?

Homo. My Lord, why may not man have hair upon his body, both as an embryo and as an adult, without being indebted for it to the lower animals? As to accounting for it, I shall be able to do so when Mr. Darwin can account satisfactorily for the fine wool-like hair which covers the tender shoots of many a giant tree when they first spring up from the ground.

Darwin. My Lord, "it appears as if the posterior molar or wisdom-teeth were tending to become rudimentary in the more civilized races of man. These teeth are rather smaller than the other molars, as is likewise the case with the corresponding teeth in the chimpanzee and the orang;

and they have only two separate fangs. They do not cut through the gums till about the seventeenth year, and I am assured by dentists that they are much more liable to decay, and are earlier lost than the other teeth. It is also remarkable that they are much more liable to vary, both in structure and in the period of their development, than the other teeth. In the Melanian races, on the other hand, the wisdom-teeth are usually furnished with three separate fangs, and are generally sound; they also differ from the other molars in size less than in the Caucasian races. Professor Schaaffhausen accounts for this difference between the races, by 'the posterior dental portion of the jaw being always shortened' in those that are civilized; and this shortening may, I presume, be safely attributed to civilized men habitually feeding on soft, cooked food, and thus using their jaws less. I am informed by Mr. Brace that it is becoming quite a common practice, in the United States, to remove some of the molar teeth of children, as the jaw does not grow large enough for the perfect development of the normal number." (Vol. i. pp. 26, 27.)

Homo. Admitting, my Lord, the correctness of Mr. Darwin's statement regarding our wisdom-teeth, I do not see that it at all helps his argument. Our teeth may resemble those of the chimpanzee or the orang, as the result of our having an animal nature like theirs, without our being blood relations of these animals. As for the teeth and jaws of civilized man becoming somewhat modified by their " habitually feeding on soft, cooked food," what has this to do, I should like to know, with our being descended from apes? No one doubts that man's physical structure is, to use Mr. Darwin's own words, "eminently variable," and that this variation arises, in part, from causes connected with our peculiar civilization. Will Mr. Darwin undertake to prove that, if man exists as the result of a separate act of creation, he either cannot possibly vary at all, or must vary in quite different directions from those in which he does vary? As for the modification of the jaw which Mr. Brace says is taking place in the United States of America, it is no doubt the result of causes in the peculiar physical conditions of the people of that country. If they had to live on nuts, and crack them with their teeth, the modification would unquestionably take another direction. The fact is, my Lord, that Mr. Darwin is reasoning here with his imagination, instead of his intellect, for in no other way than by the aid of that soaring faculty could he reach his conclusion from such premises.

Lord C. You cannot surely mean, Mr. Darwin, that the circumstance of our teeth and jaws becoming somewhat modified through our civilization proves us to be descended from the same stock with the lower animals—for that is the point you are now endeavouring to prove. Would " the younger and rising naturalists" even be satisfied with such evidence?

Homo. I should think, my Lord, none of them could, unless such as have not yet cut their wisdom-teeth.

Darwin. My Lord, " the early male progenitors of man were . . . probably furnished with great canine teeth ; but as they gradually acquired the habit of using stones, clubs, or other weapons, for fighting with their enemies, they would have used their jaws and teeth less and less. In this case, the jaws, together with the teeth, would have become reduced in size, as we may feel sure from innumerable analogous cases." (Vol. i. p. 144.)

Homo. No doubt, my Lord, if man has had such progenitors as Mr. Darwin imagines, with great canine teeth for fighting, their teeth and jaws would become reduced as they learned to fight after a more rational manner. But Mr. Darwin here takes it for granted that, in older times, brutes could manufacture "clubs" and "other weapons," which implies, of course, that they could also manufacture tools. Think of wild beasts manufacturing tools, my Lord! We shall be hearing next of manufactories set up in the dens and cages of the Zoological Gardens!

Darwin. My Lord, "he who rejects with scorn the belief that the shape of his own canines, and their occasional great development in other men, are due to our early progenitors having been provided with these formidable weapons, will probably reveal, by sneering, the line of his descent. For, though he no longer intends, nor has the power, to use these teeth as weapons, he will unconsciously retract his 'snarling muscles,' (thus named by Sir Charles Bell), so as to expose them ready for action, like a dog prepared to fight." (Vol. i. p. 127.)

Homo. Mr. Darwin is becoming very oracular, my Lord; but it would help his argument more if he could show any rational ground on which it might be believed that the canines of man, and the tusks of the wild boar, or of the elephant—a single one of which, he tells us, "has been known to weigh 180 pounds"—have been developed from the same common prototype. No intelligent person sneers when told that the earth turns on its axis, and travels with almost inconceivable rapidity in its orbit round the sun; he feels that there are good grounds on which he may believe this; but Mr. Darwin requires us to believe, without any evidence whatever, that the canine teeth of man, the tusks of hogs and elephants, and, I may add, the horns of stags and antelopes—all of them once lay concealed in the head of a tadpole!

Darwin. "This tooth," my Lord, "the canine, no longer

serves man as a special weapon for tearing his enemies or prey; it may, therefore, as far as its proper function is concerned, be considered as rudimentary." (Vol. i. p. 126.)

Homo. Mr. Darwin has not proved, my Lord—nor can he prove—that the proper function of this tooth in man is for "tearing his enemies." No one, I should think, could share this belief of Mr. Darwin but a semi-savage.

Darwin. "In every large collection of human skulls," my Lord, "some may be found, as Häckel observes, with the canine teeth projecting considerably beyond the others, in the same manner, but in a less degree, as in the anthropomorphous apes. In these cases, open spaces between the teeth in the one jaw are left for the reception of the canines belonging to the other jaw." (Vol. i. p. 126.)

Homo. That shows, my Lord, that nature works after an ideal plan. There is a typical form which she ever keeps in view.

Lord C. Mr. Darwin would, I presume, regard the cases in question as instances of "reversion to some former and ancient type of structure."

Homo. They are certainly, so far, cases of resemblance, my Lord; but when Mr. Darwin insists that the projecting canines which some few men exhibit, show reversion to a former type, he is taking for granted our descent from some brutal progenitor. Now if, at times, man were to approximate unmistakeably to the image and likeness of the brute; if he were to come into existence occasionally with "a tail and pointed ears," or with the hoofs of some quadruped, or with feet like an ape's, there would be some show of reason for this assumption. But there is certainly none in the circumstance that, now and then, a man develops a tooth which bears a remote resemblance to that of some lower animal. The fact is, my Lord, that we know far too little of the forces and materials with which Nature works, or of the laws and manner of her working, to be able to pronounce any decision in a case like this. Mr. Darwin is probably as far wrong in his statements on this point as he now acknowledges he was in what he wrote some years ago about the supernumerary mammæ of females and fingers of men.

Lord C. Pray, what was that?

Homo. Why, my Lord, in a former work he "attributed the not very rare cases of supernumerary mammæ in women to reversion, from their being generally placed symmetrically on the breast." He now finds, however, that they "have been known to occur in other situations, even on the back," by which fact, he says, " the force of my argument is greatly weakened, or perhaps entirely destroyed." (See note, Vol. i. p. 125.) It sometimes happens also that persons are born with supernumerary fingers. If they are cut off, others will grow in their stead. This also he attributed to "reversion." Unable, however, to find that there was any ancient form to which such reversion was possible, and finding " the highest authority in Europe on such a point" against him, he very candidly, though reluctantly, acknowledges himself to have been in error also on this point. "This extraordinary fact of their re-growth," he says, " remains inexplicable, if the belief in reversion to some extremely remote progenitor must be rejected." (See note, Vol. i. p. 126.) But why should he not suppose, my Lord, that " some extremely remote progenitor" occasionally had supernumerary digits? No authority could forbid him the consolation of such a belief.

Lord C. Very true; but it would not help his argument. Let us hear, however, what Mr. Darwin has to say on other points.

Darwin. "Considering," my Lord, "how few ancient skulls have been examined in comparison with recent skulls, it is an interesting fact that, in at least three cases, the canines project largely, and in the Naulette skull they are spoken of as enormous." (Vol. i. p. 126.)

Homo. I do not see, my Lord, that these cases help Mr. Darwin in the least. He is now taking it for granted that man was originally a savage. That I do not believe. I regard savages as having originated, if not in all cases, certainly in most, from some portion of our race having drained away, by its own inherent tendencies, from a higher and more genial life, to the low, wretched, death-like level at which we find it. If Mr. Darwin, therefore, could produce three hundred such skulls, instead of three, the larger development of their canines might be referred with far greater probability to degradation than to reversion.

Darwin. "To believe," my Lord, "that man was aboriginally civilized, and then suffered utter degradation in so many regions, is to take a pitiably low view of human nature." (Vol. i. pp. 184, 185.)

Homo. It is, nevertheless, a correct view. We see, unhappily, too much around us to prove its correctness. Are there not many, in all our great cities, that exhibit a tendency to sink into utter barbarism. Let them but be transported to some uninhabited island, or to some desert, and there left to themselves, and, in a very few generations, every trace of what civilization they have would disappear.

Darwin. "In the Quadrumana," my Lord, "and some other orders of animals, especially in the Carnivora, there is a passage near the lower end of the humerus called the supra-condyloid foramen, through which the great nerve of the fore-limb passes, and often the great artery. Now, in the humerus of man, as Dr. Struthers and others have shown, there is generally a trace of this passage, and it is sometimes fairly well developed, being formed by a depending hook-like process of bone, completed by a band of ligament. When present, the great nerve invariably passes through it, and this clearly indicates that it is the homologue and rudiment of the supra-condyloid foramen of the lower animals. Professor Turner estimates, as he informs me, that it occurs in about one per cent. of recent skeletons; but during ancient times it appears to have been much more common. . . . The fact that ancient races, in this and several other cases, more frequently present structures which resemble those of the lower animals, than do the modern races, is interesting. One chief cause seems to be that ancient races stand somewhat nearer than modern races in the long line of descent to their remote animal-like progenitors." (Vol. i. pp. 28, 29.)

Homo. The *Quarterly Review*, for July, says, my Lord, that Mr. Darwin "mistakes the supra-condyloid foramen of the humerus for the inter-condyloid perforation. Did the former condition frequently occur in man—as, through this mistake, Mr. Darwin asserts—it would be remarkable indeed, as it is only found in the lower monkeys, and not in the higher." (P. 64.) I leave Mr. Darwin then, to settle the account on this matter with *The Quarterly*.

Darwin. "The os coccyx in man," my Lord, "though functionless as a tail, plainly represents this part in other vertebrate animals. At an early embryonic period it is free, and, as we have seen, projects beyond the lower extremities. In certain rare and anomalous cases, it has been known, according to Isidore Geoffroy St.-Hilaire, and others, to form a small external rudiment of a tail. (Vol. i. p. 29.)

Homo. I should like, my Lord, to see the man with a tail. It is singular enough, if such a creature ever existed, that anatomists have not possessed themselves of his skeleton. We may be sure that, if one existed now, Barnum would have got hold of him long ago. Why, it would make the fortune of a showman to be able to exhibit a man with a tail. Crowds would flock to see him. He would be regarded as a curiosity even among savages.

Lord C. I fear it will not be easy to produce such a specimen of humanity. The friends of a *Homo caudatus* would be very likely to remove the appendage, unless, indeed, they meant to make capital out of the thing. I think, therefore, Mr. Darwin, you must produce either the commodity itself alive, or tangible evidence of its existence, ere we can accept the statement of the French gentleman you refer to.

Homo. I believe, my Lord, Voltaire once said that a Frenchman is a cross-breed between a tiger and a monkey.

Lord C. Meaning thereby, I presume, that the average Frenchman is too often, in character, a compound of frivolity and ferocity. But Mr. Darwin states that, "at an early embryonic period, the os coccyx projects beyond the lower extremities."

Homo. I presume, my Lord, that is because the parts that eventually surround it are not, at the early period referred to, sufficiently developed.

Darwin. "The os coccyx," my Lord, "is short, usually including only four vertebræ; and these are in a rudimental condition, for they consist, with the exception of the basal one, of the centrum alone. They are furnished with some small muscles; one of which, as I am informed by Professor Turner, has been expressly described by Theile as a rudimentary repetition of the extensor of the tail, which is so largely developed in many mammals." (Vol. i. p. 29.)

Homo. The muscles to which Mr. Darwin now refers, my Lord, have long been well known to anatomists. If what Theile says of one of them be true, the fact could not have escaped the notice of " the older and honoured chiefs in natural science." I place their judgment against that of Theile. As to the os coccyx being short, having only four vertebræ, and consisting, with the exception of the basal one, of the centrum alone, this may be quite true, but how does it prove us to be descended from apes ? Without Mr. Darwin's lively imagination, it is impossible to reach his conclusions.

Darwin. "The following fact," my Lord, "for which I am also indebted to Professor Turner, shows how closely the os coccyx corresponds with the true tail in the lower animals. Luschka has recently discovered, at the extremity of the coccygeal bones, a very peculiar convoluted body, which is continuous with the middle sacral artery ; and this discovery led Krauss and Meyer to examine the tail of a monkey (Macacus), and of a cat, in both of which they found, though not at the extremity, a similarly convoluted body. (Vol. i. p. 30.)

Homo. This, my Lord, is surely very illogical reasoning. At the extremity of the coccygeal bones a very peculiar convoluted body is found. A similar convoluted body is found in the tail of a monkey, and of a cat, though not at the extremity. Therefore man is descended from the same progenitors as the monkey and the cat ! This reasoning is about as conclusive as the specimen we had a little while ago. Some persons belonging to the same family have a few long hairs in their eyebrows, which they don't use as feelers. Cats and rats have long hairs on their upper lips and faces, which they do use as feelers. Man, therefore, is descended from the same primal stock as cats and rats! In spite, moreover, of all that Mr. Darwin has said, it is a fact that the os coccyx in man is never a tail; it has no joints; nor has it muscles that can move it, as a tail must have.

Darwin. "According to a popular impression," my Lord, "the absence of a tail is eminently distinctive of man; but as those apes that come nearest to man are destitute of this organ, its disappearance does not especially concern us. Nevertheless, it may be well to own that no explanation, as far as I am aware, has ever been given of the loss of the tail by certain apes and man." (Vol. i. p. 150.)

Lord C. That is a very candid admission.

Darwin. "Its loss, however, is not surprising," my Lord, "for it sometimes differs remarkably in length in species of the same genera. Thus, in some species of Macacus the tail is longer than the whole body, consisting of twenty-four vertebræ; in others it consists of a scarcely visible stump, containing only three or four vertebræ.... This great diversity in the structure and length of the tail in animals belonging to the same genera, and following nearly the same habits of life, renders it probable that the tail is not of much importance to them; and if so, we might have expected that it would sometimes have become more or less rudimentary, in accordance with what we incessantly see with other structures." (Vol. i. p. 150.)

Homo. Mr. Darwin, my Lord, is again reasoning on hypotheses. The length of the tail, he tells us, differs in animals belonging, not to the same species, but to the same genera, therefore it is "*probable*" that the tail is not of much importance to them; "*if so,*" we might expect it to become more or less rudimentary. This hypothetical reasoning, my Lord, is very unsatisfactory.

Lord C. True science, certainly, cannot be built upon suppositions.

Homo. Moreover, my Lord, he is accusing the god he believes to have built up the world around us—I mean Natural Selection—of the folly either of having given a tail where it was unnecessary, or of having withheld it where it should have been present. In short, he finds that Natural Selection, in giving a tail to one species of monkey, and withholding it from another similar species, has not acted consistently, nor in a way that suits his argument. I think I could suggest to Mr. Darwin a way in which he might account, consistently with his own principles, for the loss of the tail by man. He must surely, when writing on this point, have forgotten a fact regarding the larvæ of Ascidians —those representatives of our "most ancient progenitors." He knows very well that these larvæ cast off their tails when they become sessile. Why may not man have done the same when he emerged into humanity from the last of his ape-like progenitors, and thus became, if not so sessile as the Ascidian, at least more so than the ape? The loss of the tail by man might thus be attributed to "reversion to a former and ancient type of structure."

Lord C. That would be an approach to Lord Monboddo's idea, namely, "that man rubbed off his tail by sitting on it."

Darwin. My Lord, " the occurrence of such rudiments " in man, " is difficult to explain on the belief of the separate creation of each species." (Vol. i. p. 30.)

Homo. I beg to say, my Lord, that those points of similarity in bodily structure between man and the lower animals, which Mr. Darwin calls "rudiments," are sufficiently accounted for, if we regard the Creator as modelling his creatures after the same ideal plan, and bear in mind that "man is subject to much variability," and that "no two individuals of the same race are quite alike."

Darwin. "On any other view," my Lord, "than their descent from a common progenitor, together with their subsequent adaptation to diversified conditions, the similarity of pattern between the hand of a man or monkey, the foot of a horse, the flipper of a seal, the wing of a bat, &c., is utterly inexplicable. It is no scientific explanation to assert that they have all been formed on the same ideal plan." (Vol. i. pp. 31, 32.)

Homo. Allow me, my Lord, to reply to Mr. Darwin here, in the language of his reviewer in *The Times*. When Mr. Darwin says, "It is no scientific explanation to assert that they have all been formed on the same ideal plan," "he is simply begging the question. If Mr. Darwin starts with the preliminary assumption that every fact in nature is capable of scientific explanation—in other words, that no causes have ever operated except natural causes, he will, of course, reject any other causes. But this assumption is the very thing to be proved. To argue from it is to assume the whole doctrine of evolution. The assertion in question is scientific or not, according as it is true or not. The only scientific question is whether, as a matter of fact, species have been developed, by force of circumstances, out of other species, and man out of an ape. It is certainly unscientific argument to assume that they *must* have been so developed. Does the investigation of the various forms of Nature lead us up to a number of distinct points of departure? This is the question at issue. Mr. Darwin, unless he believes the world to be eternal, must admit a single point of departure, and there is nothing more essentially unscientific in the recognition of a dozen co-ordinate points of departure than in the recognition of one."

Lord C. Do you think, Mr. Darwin, that science alone will account for the existence of man? Has a Creator never intervened?

Darwin. I do not assert, my Lord, that a Creator has never intervened.

Homo. In his work on "The Origin of Species," my Lord, Mr. Darwin says, "There is a grandeur in this view of life, with its several powers, having been originally breathed by the Creator into a few forms or into one." I do not find, in his present work, any such acknowledgment of the intervention of a Creator. He says, "the idea of a universal and beneficent Creator of the universe does not seem to arise in the mind of man, until he has been elevated by long-continued culture." (Vol. ii., p. 395.) But whether or not he *now* regards this idea of a Creator as a correct one, does not appear.

Lord C. It will be but just to Mr. Darwin to regard him as retaining his formerly avowed belief in a Creator, until he expressly repudiates it.

Homo. I quite agree with your Lordship, and have certainly not the least desire to do injustice to Mr. Darwin. I cannot understand, however, why, in his present work, which seems as much as his former one to lead to the subject, he does not again indicate his belief in the intervention of the Creator. I suppose he feels that the weak point of his argument is just here. For, if he admits that the Creator must have breathed life "into a few forms," why may not man have been one of these forms? I might, besides, ask Mr. Darwin if it be a "scientific explanation" to assert that the Creator has breathed life into any form whatever? Mr. Darwin himself falls away from "scientific explanation" when he brings in the Creator.

Lord C. I quite think so, though I am glad to find Mr. Darwin's system recognizes the Creator.

Darwin. "With respect to development," my Lord, "we can clearly understand, on the principle of variations supervening at a rather late embryonic period, and being inherited at a corresponding period, how it is that the embryos of wonderfully different forms should still retain, more or less perfectly, the structure of their common progenitor." (Vol. i. p. 32.)

Lord C. You speak of "variations supervening at a rather late embryonic period, and being inherited at a corresponding period," but what proof have you that such variations ever either supervened or were inherited? Are you not here introducing a new hypothesis to sustain your old one?

Darwin. "No other explanation," my Lord, "has ever been given of the marvellous fact that the embryos of man, dog, seal, reptile, &c., can at first hardly be distinguished from each other." (Vol. i. p. 32.)

Homo. My Lord, why should Mr. Darwin make anything of this "marvellous fact," when it results from another yet more marvellous fact, which he would have us accept, viz., that the germ from which man is developed "differs in no respect from the germs of other animals." If the germs "differ in no respect," this would lead us, *à priori*, to expect that the embryos proceeding from those germs, instead of being hardly distinguishable from each other, would not be distinguished from each other at all. But this is only another of the reckless statements put forth by Mr. Darwin. Your Lordship has seen in the drawing he has supplied to us, that the embryos of man and dog, at an "early stage of development," present differences which might be pointed out by a child. Besides this, the tendencies in each germ are towards the development of the ultimate form, whatever that form may be. A dog-germ will become a dog, a bat-germ a bat, a seal-germ a seal, a reptile-germ a reptile, and a human-germ a man, in spite of Mr. Darwin and the rising naturalists. They might as well attempt to pluck the sun from the heavens as to change this order of things.

Darwin. "In order," my Lord, "to understand the existence of rudimentary organs, we have only to suppose that a former progenitor possessed the parts in question in a perfect state, and that, under changed habits of life, they became greatly reduced, either from simple disuse, or through the Natural Selection of those individuals which were least encumbered with a superfluous part, aided by the other means previously indicated." (Vol. i. p. 32.)

Lord C. That is just the difficulty, Mr. Darwin. If we suppose a former progenitor of man, we suppose your hypothesis to be true, and thus make it prove itself. We take for granted the point in dispute, in order to prove the point in dispute. This is mere reasoning in a circle. We cannot *suppose* a former progenitor until you prove this former progenitor to have really existed.

Darwin. "Thus we can understand," my Lord, "how it has come to pass that man, and all other vertebrate animals, have been constructed on the same general model, why they pass through the same early stages of development, and why they retain certain rudiments in common. Consequently, we ought frankly to admit their community of descent: to take any other view is to admit that our own structure, and that of all the animals around us, is a mere snare laid to entrap our judgment." (Vol. i. p. 32.)

Homo. I have read, my Lord, in an old book, about the " wise being taken in their own craftiness." If there be a snare in connection with this matter, it has been laid by Mr Darwin's own hand. He has allowed himself to become so enamoured of the venerable pair of hairy quadrupeds, with tails and pointed ears, from whom he thinks himself descended, that he skips over mountains more impassable than the Himalayas, and flies on the wings of imagination across separating and unfathomable abysses, that he may embrace them.

Lord C. Mr. Darwin is more probably carried away by fondness for his hypothesis. He would like to find that all animated existence has been developed from some primal form, and that there is thus a grand unity in nature. Now, there is doubtless unity in nature, but it is worthy of consideration whether it does not lie deeper than Mr. Darwin seeks it;—not in all kinds of creatures having been developed from one primal form, but in all of them having derived existence from one common source, that is, from God Himself. An over-anxious desire to find unity elsewhere than in the Creator, may become a source of error. One may thus be led to imagine there is unity where there is none, and to seek it where it cannot be found. I shall be glad to hear, at our next sitting, what Mr. Darwin has to say as to the way in which man, or rather the progenitors of man, became erect. How did the ape-like creature acquire a human-like posture?

FOURTH DAY'S SITTING.

Darwin. "As soon," my Lord, "as some ancient member in the great series of the Primates came, owing to a change in its manner of procuring subsistence, or in the conditions of its native country, to live somewhat less on trees and more on the ground, its manner of progression would have been modified; and, in this case, it would have had to become either more strictly quadrupedal or bipedal." (Vol. i. pp. 140, 141.)

Homo. My Lord, according to Mr. Darwin's hypothesis, after four-footed beasts had been developed from the primitive worm, a portion of them were changed by Natural Selection into four-handed animals, able to climb and live on trees. One would think that the monkeys must have been vain of their elevation. But Mr. Darwin now supposes them brought down from it, and changed into four-footed beasts again!

Lord C. Or into men; rather, perhaps, into man's progenitors. His words were, "quadrupedal or bipedal."

Homo. True, my Lord, and, at present, men only are bipedal. Still, the changing of two of the creature's paws from hand-feet into feet pure and simple, must have been a loss to which it would very reluctantly submit. One would think that, while the change was going on, it must have looked with regretful eyes to the trees and their tempting fruit, as it found itself becoming unable to climb them.

Lord C. You forget, Homo, that Mr. Darwin spoke of " a series of forms graduating *insensibly* from some ape-like creature to man as he now exists."

Homo. My Lord, I cannot understand this "graduating insensibly" from ape to man. Let us look at it in connection with the point now before us. Here is an "ape-like creature with tail and pointed ears," and "arboreal in its habits," for it lives on trees. The four paws which its progenitors had as quadrupeds, for carrying them along the ground, have become changed into a kind of hands with which it can clutch trunks and branches, and make its way from tree to tree with beautiful agility. Its tail also has probably, as in the case of many kinds of monkeys, became modified for twisting and grasping. Sometimes it may use its tail for balancing itself; sometimes, with easy grace, it may coil it round a branch to aid its security or assist its progress; possibly even, the extremity of its tail, like that of the spider-monkey, may have acquired a sensitiveness similar to that of the human finger, so that it may be thrust into holes in its forest haunts, in search of the eggs of birds to give an additional relish to its fruity meal. Such a creature must have been happy enough in its way. It was suited for its habitat, and its habitat was suited for it. The one answered perfectly, admirably, to the other. Can it be believed, then, that Natural Selection would have induced a change in this creature, which should have gone on sensibly, or "insensibly," through successive generations of its descendants, till they had become unfitted for their forest life, and had forsaken the trees for the ground, and their juicy fruits for such scanty roots as they might be able to grub up from the soil?

Lord C. You must remember, Homo, that Mr. Darwin supposes its living "less on trees and more on the ground," to have arisen from "a change in its manner of procuring subsistence, or in the conditions of its native country."

Homo. Mr. Darwin has a remarkable capacity for making suppositions, my Lord, but his present supposition is neither ingenuous nor ingenious. It is not ingenuous, for it is manifestly made for the purpose of helping him out of a difficulty, the existence of which he had better have frankly acknowledged. And it is not ingenious. I could myself have easily helped him to a better. Your Lordship will at once perceive that a change in the mode of this creature's procuring subsistence must have arisen from a change in the conditions of its native country. Now Africa, according to Mr. Darwin, was the native country of man's progenitors. But we know that no change of the kind supposed has taken place in Africa, for the forests of that country abound in monkeys to the present day.

Lord C. But may there not have been an era during which Africa ceased to grow forests?

Homo. There cannot have been such an era, my Lord, else, on Mr. Darwin's principles, all its monkey tribes must either have perished, or been changed either into quadrupeds or into men.

Darwin. My Lord, "Baboons frequent hilly and rocky districts, and only from necessity climb up high trees; and they have acquired almost the gait of a dog." (Vol. i. p. 141.)

Homo. It is not with tailless baboons that we are at present concerned, my Lord, but with a tailed ape, "arboreal in its habits." Will Mr. Darwin kindly keep to the point? As to baboons having "*acquired* almost the gait of a dog," can he prove that they ever had any other gait?

Darwin. "Man," my Lord, " could not have attained his present dominant position in the world without the use of his hands, which are so admirably adapted to act in obedience to his will. . . . But the hands and arms could hardly have become perfect enough to have manufactured weapons, or to have hurled stones and spears with a true aim, so long as they were habitually used for locomotion and for supporting the whole weight of the body, or as long as they were especially well adapted . . . . for climbing trees." (Vol. i. p. 141.)

Homo. Mr. Darwin, my Lord, cannot rise above the idea of man having been originally a savage, perpetually manufacturing weapons, and hurling stones and spears against his enemies. If this was the condition of his progenitors, and they had enemies against whom they required defence, one would suppose that Natural Selection would have led them to seek it in the trees on which they had been wont to make their habitation, and that so they would not have lost their power of climbing. Mr. Darwin's hypothesis is thus inconsistent and self-contradictory. Listen to it, my Lord. Man's progenitors were apes, and lived on trees. They found sustenance in their fruits, and security on their lofty branches, moving easily from one to another as they were inclined. In process of time, however, they gradually lost their power of climbing, and had to "live less on trees and more on the ground." They thus became exposed to the attacks of beasts of prey, yet, strange to say, the successive generations of them were preserved through many long eras of our earth's history, as they "gradually and insensibly" advanced in form towards man. Natural Selection thus put the heads of these poor beasts into the lion's mouth, and yet was able, somehow, to prevent the lion from biting them off!

Lord C. There might have been no lions in those imaginary times.

Homo. Possibly, my Lord, but then there would have been other kinds of brutes, quite as terrible to a poor rheumatic ape, whose hind-hands were stiffening into human feet, and which was, therefore, unable to run up a tree for security.

Darwin. "No country in the world," my Lord, "abounds in a greater degree with dangerous beasts than Southern Africa. . . . but it is quite conceivable that they (the early progenitors of man) might have existed, or even flourished, if, whilst they gradually lost their brute-like powers, such as climbing trees, &c., they at the same time advanced in intellect." (Vol. i. p. 157.)

Homo. I should say, my Lord, that it is quite *inconceivable* that the ape-like progenitors of man should have "lost their brute-like powers," especially that of climbing trees, in so dangerous a country as Southern Africa. Natural Selection would have proved a harder nurse to them than she has done even to the gorilla, had she so treated them. Then, why should she not—their circumstances being the same—have treated all the monkey tribes alike?

Darwin. "Granting," my Lord, "that the progenitors of man were far more helpless and defenceless than any existing savages, if they had inhabited some warm continent or large island, such as Australia or New Guinea, or Borneo . . . they would not have been exposed to any special danger." (Vol. i. p. 157.)

Homo. How can Mr. Darwin make such a supposition, my Lord, when he says elsewhere, "the fact that they (man's progenitors) belonged to this (the Catarhine) stock, clearly shows that they inhabited the Old World; but not Australia, nor any oceanic island, as we may infer from the laws of geographical distribution"? (Vol. i. p. 199.) This see-saw mode of reasoning might have suited man's progenitors when they were losing their brute-like powers and advancing in intellect, but it cannot be allowed now that the human and scientific era has unquestionably arrived. I have already, my Lord, mentioned one way in which, on Mr. Darwin's principles, the loss of the tail by man's progenitors might be accounted for. Allow me now to mention another. As they became unable to climb and live on trees, this appendage would become increasingly inconvenient to them. Sometimes they might be caught by it in the very act of escaping. Being thus a useless and even a dangerous article, it would gradually get into a rudimentary condition, and might eventually drop away. Or, it might have been got rid of "through the Natural Selection of those individuals who were least encumbered with a superfluous part."

Darwin. "From these causes alone," my Lord, which I have just mentioned, "it would have been an advantage to man to become a biped."

Lord C. Do you think, Mr. Darwin, that man was ever anything else than a biped? You would surely not maintain that our supposed ape-like progenitors were men?

Homo. Mr. Darwin, my Lord, often gets a little into the fog on this point. At page 235 he says, "Whether primeval man, when he possessed very few arts of the rudest kind, and when his power of language was extremely imperfect, would have deserved to be called man, must depend on the definition which we employ." He was doubtful, when writing this passage, whether man should be called "man," even when he had become somewhat endowed with speech; now, he unhesitatingly calls our progenitors "man" before they had become bipeds, and were as yet progressing on all-fours!

Darwin. I was going to add, when your Lordship interrupted me, that "for many actions it is almost necessary that both arms and the whole upper part of the body "of man" should be free; and he must, for this end, stand firmly on his feet. To gain this great advantage the feet have been rendered flat, and the great toe peculiarly modified, though this has entailed the loss of the power of prehension. . . . If it be an advantage to man to have his hands and arms free, and to stand firmly on his feet—of which there can be no doubt from his pre-eminent success in the battle of life—then I can see no reason why it should not have been advantageous to the progenitors of man to become more and more erect or bipedal." (Vol. i. pp. 141, 142.)

Lord C. In reasoning as you do, Mr. Darwin, you are begging the question in dispute. We expect you to *prove* that man has had progenitors; instead of doing so, you take it for granted! I must say, moreover, that your account of the way in which you suppose the ape to have been changed into man is far from satisfactory. It is, no doubt, "an advantage to man" to be erect and bipedal; but, that it should have been an advantage to an ape-like creature, accustomed to live on trees and find its sustenance on their produce, to lose its power of climbing them in order to attain the erect posture of man—this is, to my mind, more than doubtful. As we have already seen, and you yourself admit, it would thus have become exposed to the attacks of enemies which it would have been impossible for it to resist, and quite as impossible for it to escape. I think, therefore, you quite fail to show the possibility of such a transmutation of species as you suppose.

Darwin. My Lord, "if the gorilla and a few allied forms had become extinct, it might have been argued, with great force and apparent truth, that an animal could not have been gradually converted from a quadruped into a biped;

as all the animals in an intermediate condition would have been miserably ill-fitted for progression. But we know, and this is well worthy of reflection, that several kinds of apes are now actually in this intermediate condition; and no one doubts that they are, on the whole, well adapted for their conditions of life. Thus, the gorilla runs with a sidelong, shambling gait, but more commonly progresses by resting on its bent arms. (Vol. i. pp. 142, 143).

Homo. Here, my Lord, is an engraving of a gorilla. Though it does not show the brute as it "progresses," it gives a very fair idea of its general appearance. Your Lordship is aware that the gorilla belongs to the stem of the Old World monkeys from which, Mr. Darwin tells us, "man proceeded," and is now one of our "nearest allies."

Lord C. Perhaps it may be my moderate acquaintance with the science of Natural History, but I am unable to recognize the relationship. Will Mr. Darwin proceed?

Darwin. "The long-armed apes," my Lord, occasionally use their arms like crutches, swinging their bodies forward between them; and some kinds of Hylobates, without having been taught, can run or walk upright with tolerable quickness, yet they move awkwardly and much less securely than man. We see, in short, with existing monkeys, various gradations between a form of progression strictly like that of a quadruped, and that of a biped or man." (Vol. i. p. 143.)

Lord C. But is not that just what we might expect, Mr. Darwin? As monkeys are, in outward form, intermediate between quadrupeds and man, and are, moreover, as you tell us, "on the whole, well adapted for their conditions of life," you surely do not mean to maintain that they were ever better adapted, or less adapted, for their conditions of life, and are actually, now, undergoing a process of

The Gorilla, now one of our "nearest allies"!

transformation. Yet your language sounds ambiguously. If, however, you mean to assert, for example, that the gorilla ever ran or progressed in a way different from that in which it "runs" or "progresses" now, I must call on you to prove your assertion.

Homo. A vain call that would be, my Lord. Mr. Darwin would only furnish your Lordship with another curious specimen of reasoning. When Mr. Darwin is reasoning—will your Lordship pardon the remark?—he reminds me of those apes he has been speaking of, which use their long arms like crutches, swinging their bodies forward between them. The premises that Mr. Darwin reasons from are certainly not facts, but merely monkey-like crutches. He plants them, however, as firmly as he can on some imaginary basis, and then swings himself forward between them, through all the acknowledged laws of human science and logic, to the position he wishes to occupy. Mr. Darwin's intellectual movements, my Lord, in conducting the reasoning process, are far more ungainly than those bodily movements of the gorilla which he has just described. Natural Selection, my Lord, may have endowed Mr. Darwin with considerable power of imagination, and with a capacious memory for the facts of Natural History, but she has certainly denied him the gift of being able to reason justly, and that yet higher gift—the true spirit of philosophy—which, as your Lordship remarked, is just a "sincere love of truth."

Lord C. Have you anything to say, Mr. Darwin, regarding the size of the brain in man compared with its size in the lower animals?

Darwin. My Lord, "Dr. J. Barnard Davis has proved by many careful measurements, that the mean internal capacity of the skull in Europeans is 92·3 cubic inches; in Americans,

87·5; in Asiatics, 87·1; and in Australians only 81·9 inches." (Vol. i. p. 146.)

Lord C. That is not the point about which I enquire. I ask, What is the size of the brain in man compared with its size in the lower animals—in the ape, for example?

Homo. Mr. Darwin, my Lord, gives no answer to that question. He merely mentions some trifling facts about the size of the brains and skulls of domestic rabbits, and tells us how disease may modify the shape of the skull in man. But Mr. Wallace mentions, at page 338 of "Contributions to the theory of Natural Selection," that the proportions are "represented by the following figures—anthropoid apes, 10; savages, 26; civilized man, 32." Mr. Wallace remarks (page 342) that man is able to "form and use weapons and implements which are beyond the physical power of brutes; but having done this, he certainly does not exhibit more mind in using than do many lower animals. What is there in the life of the savage (he asks), but the satisfying of the cravings of appetite in the simplest and easiest way? What thoughts, ideas, or actions are there, that raise him many grades above the elephant or the ape? Yet he possesses, as we have seen, a brain vastly superior to theirs in size and complexity; and this brain gives him, in an undeveloped state, faculties which he never requires to use."

Lord C. These are most important considerations.

Homo. My Lord, a writer in *The Edinburgh Review* for July, 1871, page 204, remarks on this: "It is clear, therefore, that the brain of savage man is far beyond his needs. How can this be accounted for by the principle of Natural Selection, or by the accumulation of small variations good for the individual? The large size" of the brain of the savage "cannot be traced to circumstances of life, because it is quite disproportionate to the actual requirement; and even if once originated, it ought, according to Mr. Darwin's theory, to have been lost by disuse. For if Natural Selection tends in some instances to raise a race of beings, it might tend in others to lower it. To a savage, the organs and instincts of an animal might be more useful than the latent brain power of a sage."

Lord C. And yet the savage often has the latent brain power of the sage! Mr. Darwin should tell us how the savage has acquired this power, seeing that he could not have inherited it either from his savage or from his ape-like progenitors.

Homo. It would have been more to the purpose, my Lord, for Mr. Darwin to have tried to reconcile these facts with his hypothesis, than for him to have entertained us with the fancy pictures he has just been exhibiting.

Lord C. I fear he would then have been attempting an impossibility.

Homo. It has been remarked, my Lord, that the title of Mr. Darwin's book is a misnomer, and that it should have been, not "The Descent of Man," but "The Ascent of Man." I think it should rather have been, "The Evolution of Man from a Tadpole taken for granted, and the steps by which 'we may confidently believe' it came about."

FIFTH DAY'S SITTING.

Lord C. Will Mr. Darwin now inform us what further evidence he has to offer in support of his hypothesis?

Darwin. Your Lordship has already heard the whole of the evidence I have to adduce in support of the views which I maintain regarding the origin of man. That evidence is exhausted in the first two-and-twenty pages of my book! The first chapter is entitled, "*The evidence of the descent of man from some lower form.*" In the second and third chapters I compare *the mental powers of man and the lower animals.* The fourth chapter is *On the manner of development of man from some lower form.* The fifth chapter, *On the development of the intellectual and moral faculties, during primeval and civilized times.* The sixth, *On the affinities and genealogy of man.* Chapter seventh is *On the races of man.* I then proceed, in the second part of my work, to the subject of Sexual Selection, which occupies the remainder of the first volume and nearly the whole of the second. In this part I speak mostly of changes which I suppose sexual preference to have introduced into the animal kingdom.

Lord C. It will not be necessary for us to hear you on that portion of your work, inasmuch as we have to do only with your assertions as to man's descent from some lower form.

Homo. May I, however, call your Lordship's attention to the fact that, while Mr. Darwin tries to account for the many forms of beauty that meet the eye among living creatures around us, by what he calls Sexual Selection, he leaves unaccounted for the fact that we find quite as many and as wonderful forms of beauty in the floral world, where Sexual Selection can have no play. For I suppose that flowers, in producing their kind, exercise no preference as to their partners.

Lord C. From which I suppose you infer that, while Sexual Selection may have something to do in modifying the creatures among whom it comes into play, Mr. Darwin makes too much of it, and attributes to it a power which it does not possess.

Homo. That is precisely what I think, my Lord. I do not believe that Sexual Selection, even with the aid of Natural Selection, could have raised, from the tadpole offspring of a worm, the forms of beauty which meet the eye everywhere in the world of living things around us—among insects, fishes, birds, reptiles, and mammals.

Lord C. I suppose the next point that claims attention is the mental and moral powers possessed by man, and the seemingly impassable gulf fixed, by his possessing those powers, between him and the lower animals. How does Mr. Darwin treat this part of his subject?

Homo. Most unsatisfactorily, my Lord. We might expect that, in attempting, as he does, to prove that the mental powers of man and animals are the same in *kind*, and differ only in respect of development, he would begin by giving us a minute and careful analysis of those powers. He does not seek even so far to enlighten us. Without having kindled any torch to guide either himself or his readers, he heedlessly plunges into what men of the highest intellect have always felt to be a great and mysterious deep, to be explored, therefore, with awe and reverence. He manages, however, after a most uncomfortable fashion, to flounder his way through it, but not without giving one the impression that he is more at home in studying the instincts and habits of the beasts of the earth than in discussing the wondrous nature and noble faculties of man.

Lord C. Does he not define and explain what he means by instinct and reason, and endeavour to point out the separating line between them?

Homo. He does nothing of the sort, my Lord. In his work on "The Origin of Species," however, referring to instinct, he says, "An action which we ourselves should require experience to enable us to perform, when performed by an animal, more especially by a very young one, and when performed by many individuals in the same way, without their knowing for what purpose it is performed, is usually said to be instinctive." To this he adds, "I could show that none of these characters of instinct are universal. A little dose, as Pierre Huber expresses it, of judgment or reason often comes into play, even in animals low in the scale of nature." (Pp. 256, 257.)

Lord C. Here we feel our need of definition. What does Mr. Darwin mean by "reason"? Does he mean such reason, or reasoning power, as man possesses? Many contend that the lower animals—dogs, for instance—possess an inferior kind of reason, which helps, in some cases, to guide them. When, for example, they have to decide to which of two contending instincts they shall yield, some would say that it is by an inferior kind of reason that they decide; others, that it is the more powerful instinct that sways them. When, again, they imitate the actions of man, apparently to accomplish a certain end, *e. g.*, the opening of a door—a dog will use his paws for this purpose—it will be said by some that they act from an inferior kind of reason. Now, even granting that in such cases a dog acts from a principle higher than instinct, which principle may be called *reason*, such reason is certainly very different from the reason that influences a man when he compares ideas, weighs motives, prepares for the future, determines on some course of action, or engages in the study of Philosophy or of Natural History. We cannot conceive such faculties as a dog possesses, however highly developed, turned to such subjects as those on which man employs his faculties habitually. But I will now hear what Mr. Darwin has to advance as evidence that the mental and moral powers of man may have arisen by development from the faculties of the lower animals.

Darwin. "No doubt," my Lord, "the difference in this respect," respect of mental power, "is enormous, even if we compare the mind of one of the lowest savages, who has no words to express any number higher than four, and who uses no abstract terms for the commonest objects or affections, with that of the most highly organised ape. The difference would, no doubt, still remain immense, even if one of the higher apes had been improved or civilized as much as a dog has been, in comparison with its parent form, the wolf or jackal. The Fuegians rank among the lowest barbarians; but I was continually struck with surprise how closely the three natives on board H.M.S. "Beagle," who had lived some years in England and could talk a little English, resembled us in disposition, and in most of our mental faculties." (Vol. i. p. 34.)

Homo. He supposes, my Lord, that it would be possible for us to improve and civilize an ape as we can a dog. Now, it is clear that the dog may be improved, and, in a certain sense, civilized, but we have no evidence that the ape can. Had the civilizing of this creature been possible, it would, doubtless, long ago have been adopted as a pet by the ladies. An ape might spend its lifetime in our country without acquiring one word of English, and it will be long before Mr. Darwin will be able to train one to resemble us either in disposition or mental faculty.

Lord C. So far, then, Mr. Darwin has been but indicating a boundary line which no one of the inferior animals ever has crossed, while a savage can cross it easily. The difference here, even between a savage and any animal, may, not improperly, be said to be infinite. What Mr. Darwin says of the Fuegians, who "rank among the lowest barbarians," is most important, viz., that, " after they had lived some years in England, and had acquired a little of our language, he was continually struck with surprise at how closely they resembled us in disposition and in most of our mental faculties."

Homo. That clearly shows, my Lord, that the mental faculties of man are not inherited, as, on Mr. Darwin's hypothesis, they should be. From whom could the Fuegians have inherited their mental powers? According to Mr. Darwin, if we go back from any savage race in the line of its progenitors, we shall find it savage still. Yet it is a fact that, though they may not exercise them, savage races possess all the mental powers of civilized races. But they cannot have become possessed of them through Natural Selection and the laws of inheritance, for, on Mr. Darwin's supposition, their progenitors never exercised those powers. Here, as it seems to me, Mr. Darwin contradicts and disproves his own hypothesis.

Lord C. Clearly so. According to Mr. Darwin's hypothesis the faculties man now possesses should have been gradually acquired by man's progenitors through Natural Selection, and transmitted by inheritance to his posterity.

According to facts observed and recorded by Mr. Darwin, those faculties are possessed by savages who "rank among the lowest barbarians," and who could therefore have had no progenitors who exercised those faculties, or were capable of transmitting them!

Homo. Thus, my Lord, as with the brain of savage man, so also with his mental powers. Mr. Darwin is utterly unable, on his hypothesis, to account for the savage possessing them. If we suppose, with Mr. Darwin, that the savage is descended from savage progenitors, the fact of his possessing a brain—and mental powers which he could not possibly have inherited from those progenitors, seeing they never possessed them—this fact would show that the savage was made for a far higher condition of life than that which he occupies. Though he himself is not aware of it, and though his progenitors could not possibly have imagined such a thing, the savage possesses an intellect capable of ranging through the universe, and penetrating into the deepest secrets of nature. Now, Divine purpose could have given him such an intellect, but, certainly, Natural Selection could not.

Lord C. From which, I suppose, you would infer, either that the savage is descended from an ancestry superior to himself, and has sunk from a higher position into a lower one; or that he was created that he might occupy a far higher level of life than that on which we find him.

Homo. Precisely so, my Lord, but either supposition is opposed to Mr. Darwin's hypothesis.

Lord C. What is the next point?

Darwin. "If no organic being, excepting man," my Lord, "had possessed any mental power, or if his powers had been of a wholly different nature from those of the lower animals, then we should never have been able to convince ourselves that our high faculties had been gradually developed. But it can be clearly shown that there is no fundamental difference of this kind. We must also admit that there is a much wider interval, in mental power, between one of the lowest fishes, as a lamprey or lancelet, and one of the higher apes, than between an ape and a man; yet this immense interval is filled up by numberless gradations." (Vol. i. pp. 34, 35.)

Homo. The lamprey, or stone-sucker, my Lord, is a kind of eel which attaches itself by the mouth to stones or rocks, to prevent the tide or current from carrying it away. This I hold to be a very sensible operation on its part, and one that man himself, in a similar difficulty, might perform with advantage. The lancelet is a similar kind of fish, smaller in size. These creatures have just the amount of instinct, or "mental power"—if Mr. Darwin prefers calling it so—which they require. Perhaps, if Mr. Darwin were to take some pains with a lamprey, he might, to some extent, succeed in improving, or even in civilizing it—which is more than he can do with an ape; but he would be unable to teach either the one or other to talk English, or count four, or understand an abstract term; nor could he bring them to resemble us in disposition and mental faculty. This of itself is sufficient to prove that the interval, in mental power, between either of them and man, is practically infinite. It is the merest folly, then, to compare them with man. But this is only another of the follies to which Mr. Darwin is driven by the stress of his argument.

Lord C. Mr. Darwin says that "there is no fundamental difference," in mental faculty, between man and the lower animals. Does he explain what he means by a "fundamental difference?"—what, in his view, would constitute such a difference?

Homo. My Lord, Mr. Darwin says that his object, in the second chapter of his work, "is solely to show that there is no fundamental difference between man and the higher mammals in their mental faculties," but he nowhere tells us what he would regard as such a difference. He maintains, however, that man's faculties do not differ *in kind* from those of the lower animals, and that man's superiority arises entirely from his being more perfectly developed.

Lord C. Development, then, alone, is to account for man's superiority.

Homo. Just so, my Lord. The lofty faculties of man were once in embryo in a thing like a tadpole! The mind of Newton once lay hid in a creature which "hardly appeared like an animal"—which consisted merely of "a simple, tough, leathery sac, with two small projecting orifices," and which stuck to a rock or bit of seaweed that it might not be carried away by the tide. Then, my Lord, as to the development which Mr. Darwin thinks would turn the faculties of a brute into human reason, we have no evidence that it is a possible thing.

Lord C. Mr. Darwin has certainly adduced none. It will not be necessary for us to consider the instincts which are common to man with the lower animals. You admit, I suppose, Homo, that there are many points in which those instincts resemble one another?

Homo. Unquestionably, my Lord. Man has an animal nature, like the inferior creatures around him, and must consequently, in many respects, resemble them. The question is, whether man has not also a higher nature which they do not partake of, and cannot comprehend, and with which they can have no sympathy. We may therefore pass by what Mr. Darwin says on "instincts which are common to man with the lower animals." I might object to statements he makes regarding " the emotions, curiosity, imitation, memory," &c., but we had better proceed at once to what he refers to as points in which man is supposed to differ essentially from all other animals.

Lord C. Will Mr. Darwin mention what these points are?

Darwin. " It has been asserted," my Lord, " that man alone is capable of progressive improvement ; that he alone makes use of tools or fire ; domesticates other animals ; possesses property, or employs language ; that no other animal is self-conscious, comprehends itself, has the power of abstraction, or possesses general ideas ; that man alone has a sense of beauty, is liable to caprice, has the feeling of gratitude, mystery, &c. ; believes in God, or is endowed with a conscience. I will hazard a few remarks on the more important and interesting of these points. Archbishop Sumner formerly maintained that man alone is capable of progressive improvement." (Vol. i. p. 49.)

Homo. It is clear, my Lord, that by "progressive improvement," the Archbishop meant *indefinite* progressive improvement. He meant that man has gone on advancing, as Mr. Darwin himself admits, from the earliest dawn of his existence until now ; and that there is apparently no limit to his capacity for advancement. Man alone inherits, and is able to use, the accumulated knowledge of the past, and to transmit it augmented to the future.

Lord C. Precisely so ; Mr. Darwin himself cannot doubt this.

Darwin. My Lord, "every one who has had experience in setting traps, knows that young animals can be caught more easily than old ones ; and they can be much more easily approached by an enemy. Even with respect to old animals, it is impossible to catch many in the same place, and in the same kind of trap, or to destroy them by the same kind of poison; yet it is improbable that all should have partaken of the poison, and impossible that all should have been caught in the trap. They must learn caution by seeing their brethren caught or poisoned... If we look to successive generations, or to the race, there is no doubt that birds and other animals gradually both acquire, and lose, caution in relation to man or other enemies; and this caution is certainly, in chief part, an inherited habit or instinct, but, in part, the result of individual experience. ... Our domestic dogs ... have progressed in certain moral qualities, such as affection, trustworthiness, temper, and probably in general intelligence. The common rat has conquered and beaten several other species throughout Europe, in parts of North America, New Zealand, and recently in Formosa, as well as on the mainland of China. Mr. Swinhoe, who describes these latter cases, attributes the victory of the common rat to its superior cunning; and this latter quality may be attributed to the habitual exercise of all its faculties in avoiding extirpation by man, as well as to nearly all the less cunning or weak-minded rats having been successively destroyed by him. To maintain, independently of any direct evidence, that no animal, during the course of ages, has progressed in intellect, or other mental faculties, is to beg the question of the evolution of species." (Vol. i. pp. 49, 51.)

Lord C. It may be quite true, Mr. Darwin, that the instinct of self-preservation in birds, and rats, and other animals, may become more or less keen as it is more or less exercised, but you surely cannot mean that this circumstance shows them to be capable of indefinite improvement, and to possess the same kind of mental powers that man possesses

Homo. Pray, observe, my Lord, the singular way in which Mr. Darwin reasons. He is replying to Archbishop Sumner's remark, "that man alone is capable of progressive improvement," meaning, clearly enough, such an improvement as has been going on among men for thousands of years, is going on now, and, for aught we can tell, may go on for ever. In reply to this, Mr. Darwin urges that the common rat is superior in cunning to other rats, and that it *may* owe this superiority to the habitual exercise of all its faculties in avoiding extirpation by man. He thus makes the supposed improvement of an instinct in rats to be parallel to the advancement of the whole human race in knowledge. The Archbishop says, "Man alone of all animals is capable of indefinite progressive improvement, and therefore differs in faculty from all other animals." Mr. Darwin replies, "The common rat is superior in cunning to all other rats, and may perhaps have become so through contact with man; the common rat, therefore, is capable of indefinite, progressive improvement." This, surely, is reasoning with the imagination. Mr. Darwin talks of our "begging the question of the evolution of species"! He is begging it himself by such reasoning.

Lord C. You say, Mr. Darwin, that "the superior cunning of the rat may be attributed to the exercise of all its faculties to avoid being extirpated by man." Will you mention the faculties it has exercised to this end? I should like to know what faculties, in addition to its five senses, you ascribe to the rat.

Homo. Mr. Darwin does not go so minutely into his subject as your Lordship's question supposes. Probably, however, he would say that, in addition to the usual senses, a rat has memory, perhaps also curiosity, imitation, attention, imagination, and reason. He supposes other animals to possess these faculties; then, why not the rat?

Lord C. Mr. Darwin speaks of the dog having "progressed in affection, trustworthiness, temper, and probably in general intelligence." Does he try to show that the dog of to-day is in advance of the dog of a thousand years ago in these qualities?

Homo. Mr. Darwin, my Lord, does not attempt to show that the dog has advanced. I believe it would be impossible for him to show that any animal whatever, from the Ascidian up to the ape has advanced, unless it be those that have done so through the skill and care of man himself, or by their otherwise coming into contact with him.

Lord C. On this point, then, we come to the conclusion that, while certain of the lower animals are capable of improvement in some of their instincts or faculties, within a certain limited range, we have no proof that any of them are capable of *indefinite progressive* improvement as man is. What is the next point?

Darwin. "The Duke of Argyll remarks," my Lord, "that the fashioning of an implement for a special purpose is absolutely peculiar to man; and he considers that this forms an unmeasurable gulf between him and the brutes. It is no doubt a very important distinction, but there appears to me much truth in Sir J. Lubbock's suggestion, that when primeval man first used flint stones for any purpose, he would have accidentally splintered them, and would then have used the sharp fragments. From this step it would be a small one to intentionally break the flints, and not a very wide step to rudely fashion them." (Vol. i. pp. 52, 53.)

Lord C. Granting what you say to be true, Mr. Darwin, it neither closes, nor bridges over, the gulf between man and the brute to which the Duke refers. Apes have existed quite as long as man, but no one of them has ever taken the steps in question, nor, so far as I can see, is ever likely to do so.

Darwin. "It has often been said," my Lord, "that no animal uses any tool; but the chimpanzee, in a state of nature, cracks a native fruit, somewhat like a walnut, with a stone." (Vol. i. p. 51.)

Lord C. If the chimpanzee does so now, he has doubtless done so for thousands of years. How is it that, during all that time, he has not learned to fashion a tool for breaking nuts, and that he cannot supply you with this proof of his possessing mental qualities like those of man?

Homo. And how is it, my Lord, that even Mr. Darwin himself cannot teach an ape to fashion a tool? The brute is too obstinate for him. Yet he talks of animals, during the course of ages, progressing in intellect! Will he undertake to teach an ape or any kind of monkey, or any animal whatever, the use of fire?

Lord C. I presume Mr. Darwin will rather decline the task.

Homo. Why should he, my Lord, if, as he maintains, animals are capable of progressive improvement?

Lord C. I shall be glad, however, to know what Mr. Darwin does say on this point—the fact that man alone makes use of fire.

Homo. He says nothing about it whatever, my Lord—a circumstance which I can account for only by supposing that he is as much afraid of fire, in connection with this subject, as an anthropomorphous ape would be afraid of fire, were it consuming the tree in which it has sought refuge.

Lord C. Then I must say that Mr. Darwin gives the

"go-by" to a most important branch of evidence which tells strongly against his hypothesis. He has himself mentioned the fact that man alone makes use of fire.

Homo. Very true, my Lord. He also refers repeatedly to the fact of man having "*discovered* the art of making fire," but he says nothing of the farther fact that no one of the lower animals has either discovered, or can be taught to use this element.

Lord C. What comes next?

Darwin. "The anthropomorphous apes," my Lord, "guided probably by instinct, build for themselves temporary platforms; but, as many instincts are largely controlled by reason, the simpler ones, such as this of building a platform, might readily pass into a voluntary and conscious act." (Vol. i. p. 53.)

Homo. Here, again, my Lord, Mr. Darwin is dealing, not with facts, but with probabilities. The apes of which he speaks were "guided *probably* by instinct;" this instinct *might* pass into "a voluntary and conscious act." There is nothing certain here, my Lord. Mr. Darwin is again using his imagination in reasoning with us. Besides, if the instinct of an ape, in building a platform, *might* pass into a voluntary and conscious act, might not the instinct of a bird in building a nest do the same; or the instinct of a mole in burrowing in the ground?

Darwin. "The orang," my Lord, "is known to cover itself at night with the leaves of the pandanus; and Brehm states that one of his baboons used to protect itself from the heat of the sun by throwing a straw mat over its head. In these latter habits we probably see the first steps towards some of the simpler arts, namely, rude architecture and dress, as they arose amongst the early progenitors of man." (Vol. i. p. 53.)

Lord C. It would be to some purpose if Mr. Darwin could show that the orang's covering itself with leaves is a *recent* invention on its part?

Homo. I have known a dog, my Lord, to work its way under straw, and even under a blanket, to keep itself warm in cold weather, and it is well known that cattle will seek the shade of trees as a screen from the heat of the sun. As for the baboon, we may regard it as taking a first step in architecture when it *makes* the straw mat for the purpose of screening itself from the heat, or improves on this method of protection by some new invention of its own.

Lord C. How is it if the orang has taken a first step in architecture, that it does not proceed to take a second?

Homo. And how is it, my Lord, that even man himself cannot teach the brute to do so? But Mr. Darwin has no answer for such questions.

Lord C. What have you to say, then, Mr. Darwin, regarding language?

Darwin. "Articulate language," my Lord, "is peculiar to man; but he uses, in common with the lower animals, inarticulate cries to express his meaning, aided by gestures and the movements of the muscles of the face." (Vol. i. p. 54.)

Homo. I presume, my Lord, it is to articulate language you are now referring, and not to the inarticulate cries either of man or animal. The question is not whether man has certain instincts and powers corresponding with those of the lower animals. No one doubts that. In so far as man is an animal, he must, of course, have qualities resembling those of animals. But the question is whether man, while an animal, is not also more than an animal, and whether, therefore, he does not possess powers which no animal either does or can possess. Mr. Darwin is leading us away from the point when he talks about the inarticulate cries of man and animals. Let him tell us whether any creature on this earth, except man, can rationally use, or be taught rationally to use, articulate language.

Darwin. "It is not the mere power of articulation," my Lord, "that distinguishes man from other animals, for, as every one knows, parrots can talk; but it is his large power of connecting definite sounds with definite ideas; and this obviously depends on the development of the mental faculties." (Vol. i. p. 54.)

Lord C. That is just the point, Mr. Darwin; let us therefore confine ourselves to it. Of course, parrots may be taught to utter a few articulate sounds, and so may starlings. But the question is, Do any of the lower animals possess "man's large power of connecting definite sounds with definite ideas?" Can you mention one that has this power, or in which it may certainly be developed?

Homo. You will not find it easy, my Lord, to hold Mr. Darwin to the point. He knows very well what the point is, for he states it clearly enough; but he no sooner does so than he starts away from it like a scared animal, and never ventures to look near it again. Would you believe it, my Lord? He gives us nine pages on language, without once attempting to discuss in them that peculiarity which, he says, distinguishes man from other animals—"his large power of connecting definite sounds with definite ideas."

Lord C. What then are the points he takes up?

Homo. He tells us, my Lord, that the dog barks in four or five different tones, to express so many different feelings that may influence him; that the sounds uttered by birds offer, in several respects, the nearest analogy to language; and he gives details which he thinks shows that an instinctive tendency to acquire an art is not a peculiarity confined to man. All this, your Lordship will at once perceive, falls far short of the mark. He then gives us a dissertation on the origin of articulate language; tells us that "some early progenitor of man *probably* used his voice largely, as does one of the gibbon-apes of the present day, in producing musical cadences;" that "monkeys certainly understand much that is said to them by man," and "utter signal cries of danger to their fellows;" and, in this, he finds what would have been "a first step in the formation of a language." (Vol. i. pp. 54-57.)

Lord C. What are Mr. Darwin's own words on this point?

Darwin. "As monkeys in a state of nature," my Lord, "utter signal cries of danger to their fellows, it does not appear altogether incredible that some unusually wise ape-like animal should have thought of imitating the growl of a beast of prey, so as to indicate to his fellow monkeys the nature of the expected danger. And this would have been a first step in the formation of a language." (Vol. i. p. 57.)

Homo. It is rather singular, my Lord, that this "unusually wise ape-like animal," which Mr. Darwin cannot prove ever existed, but to which, nevertheless, the thought occurred of imitating the growl of a beast of prey, to warn his fellow monkeys of danger, should not have thought also of imitating the hiss of the serpent, to intimate to them the proximity of that reptile, of which, according to Mr. Darwin, monkeys have an instinctive dread. The organs of an ape are as fit for hissing as for growling.

Darwin. "As the voice," my Lord, "was used more and more, the vocal organs would have been strengthened and perfected through the principle of the inherited effects of use; and this would have reacted on the power of speech. But the relation between the continued use of language, and the development of the brain, has no doubt been far more important. The mental powers, in some early progenitor of man, must have been more highly developed than in any existing ape, before even the most imperfect form of speech could have come into use; but we may confidently believe that the continued use and advancement of this power would have reacted on the mind by enabling and encouraging it to carry on long trains of thought." (Vol. i. p. 57.)

Homo. In this passage, your Lordship will perceive that Mr. Darwin takes for granted what he cannot prove—viz., that man had ape-like progenitors, and that some one of them possessed mental powers more highly developed than those of any existing ape. Reasoning from this highly-developed, hypothetical ape, he tells us that, by exercising what power of utterance it had, the brain enlarged and the mind improved, and the vocal organs strengthened, generation after generation, till this series of changes in a race of apes culminated in man! But all this is purely imaginary. Mr. Darwin cannot produce even the shadow of a proof that this "unusually wise ape-like animal" ever existed to transmit his wisdom to his descendants, or that he had descendants to inherit it. Yet he tells us we may "confidently believe" it! Instead of trying to prove to us that such development has occurred, he asks us "confidently to believe" that it has occurred!

Lord C. Mr. Darwin certainly reasons very strangely. It is a singular circumstance, moreover, that, if the "unusually wise ape-like animal" which he supposes took the first step in the formation of a language, ever really existed, there should not have arisen other "unusually wise" apes to take farther steps in the same direction, so that there should have been speaking apes at the present day. But no existing race of apes seems to have got beyond the "growl" of which Mr. Darwin has spoken.

Homo. Nor even so far as that, my Lord. No existing race of apes ever had this "unusually wise" progenitor to teach them to imitate the growl of a beast of prey to warn their "brethren" of danger. Only the race which developed into man was so favoured!

Lord C. What follows after this?

Homo. Mr. Darwin goes on, my Lord, through page after page, telling us, among other things as little to the point, that, "as Horne Tooke observes, language is an art, like brewing or baking," and not an instinct; that "the sounds uttered by birds offer in several respects the nearest analogy to language," and what he "cannot doubt" as to the origin of language; that ants communicate among themselves "by means of their antennæ;" that "we might have used our fingers" for speech, but that the loss of our hands, while thus employed, would have been a serious inconvenience; that "the fact of the higher apes not using their vocal organs for speech, no doubt results from their intelligence not being sufficiently advanced;" that, in this respect, they are like those "birds which possess organs fitted for singing, though they never sing;" and that the crow has "vocal organs similarly constructed" to those of the nightingale, though it uses them merely for "croaking." He thus wanders from one unimportant point to another, always avoiding the real point, and then winds up as follows:—"From these few and imperfect remarks I conclude that the extremely complex and regular construction of many barbarous languages, is no proof that they owe their origin to a special act of creation. Nor, as we have seen, does the faculty of articulate speech, in itself, offer any insuperable objection to the belief that man has been developed from some lower form." (Vol. i. p. 62.) Now, the question, my Lord, is, not whether languages owe their origin to a separate act of creation, but whether any inferior animal possesses "man's large power of connecting definite sounds with definite ideas." Moreover, when Mr. Darwin says that "the faculty of articulate speech, in itself," does not "offer any insuperable objection to the belief that man has been developed from some lower form," he is begging the question in dispute.

Lord C. Clearly so. Put in another form, the question at present is, Does not man's possession of the faculty of articulate speech offer an insuperable objection to the belief that he has been developed from some lower form?

Homo. Mr. Darwin, my Lord, ventures to say, " we have seen that it does not;" but we have seen nothing of the kind. Here again his imagination comes into play. First he imagines a thing; then he thinks he sees it; then, that others see it as well as himself. Finally, he writes it down as a scientific fact, and thus builds up his hypothesis.

Lord C. What points come next?

Darwin. "*Self-consciousness*," my Lord; "*Individuality, Abstraction, General Ideas, &c.* It would be useless to attempt discussing these high faculties, which, according to several recent writers, make the sole and complete distinction between man and the brutes, for hardly two authors agree in their definitions. Such faculties could not have been fully developed in man until his mental powers had advanced to a high standard, and this implies the use of a perfect language." (Vol. i. p. 62.)

Homo. If Mr. Darwin, my Lord, had wished to discuss these faculties, he might easily have found definitions which would have answered the purpose. But, after giving us *nine* pages on language, without coming to the point, he gives us *one* page on "these high faculties" which, he tells us, "several recent writers make the sole and complete distinction between man and the brutes." This looks more like again avoiding a difficulty than boldly meeting it. Will your Lordship observe, also, that here again Mr. Darwin is begging the question he professes to discuss? He takes it for granted that man's mental powers were gradually developed, which is just the point now in debate. He thus, as usual, tries to prove his hypothesis by assuming it to be true.

Lord C. It would be more satisfactory, certainly, if Mr. Darwin would bring forward proof of the gradual development of man's mental powers. But it would be difficult to show that we moderns, notwithstanding all the advantages we unquestionably have over the ancients, possess loftier mental powers than were displayed by them. Mr. Darwin will not venture to say that Homer, Plato, Aristotle, and many others, were not, in this respect, fully abreast of ourselves.

Darwin. "No one supposes," my Lord, "that one of the lower animals reflects whence he comes or whither he goes—what is death or what is life—and so forth. But can we feel sure that an old dog, with an excellent memory and some power of imagination, as shown by his dreams, never reflects on his past pleasures in the chase? and this would be a form of self-consciousness. On the other hand, as Büchner has remarked, how little can the hard-worked wife of a degraded Australian savage, who uses hardly any abstract words, and cannot count above four, exert her self-consciousness, or reflect on the nature of her own existence!" (Vol. i. p. 52.)

Lord C. If your hypothesis is to stand, Mr. Darwin, it

must be sustained by facts. Now, you are not stating a fact when you ask, " Can we feel sure that an old dog never reflects on his past pleasures in the chase ?" You yourself merely *suppose* he does, but are evidently not certain of it.

Homo. Mr. Darwin is thus unable, my Lord, even when taking the argument his own way, to find self-consciousness in a dog. The huntsman is self-conscious when he recalls the events of the chase, and the part he himself took in it, and discusses them with his friends; but can Mr. Darwin himself imagine a hound remembering the circumstances even of yesterday's chase, and reasoning on them with his fellow hounds ? Has he ever seen a pack of hounds conferring together on the events of the chase when it is over, each showing himself conscious, by the tone in which he barks, of the part he has had in it ? As to the hard-worked wife of the Australian savage, Mr. Darwin does not venture to deny to her, degraded though she be, the power of exerting self-consciousness, and reflecting on her own existence. Even granting that she uses hardly any abstract words, and cannot count above four, the fact that she does use *some* abstract words, and *can* count four, is sufficient to prove that she possesses the power of *abstraction*, and can form *general ideas*. She can also do what Mr. Darwin tells us no one of the lower animals can do—she can reflect on " whence she comes and whither she goes—what is death and what is life, and so forth." We have here then, on Mr. Darwin's own showing, even in the lowest form of savage life, all the high faculties of which he speaks,—*Self-consciousness, Abstraction, General Ideas*, and also *Individuality*, for the others imply this; but Mr. Darwin fails to show even the dawn of any one of these faculties in any brute whatever.

Darwin. My Lord, "that animals retain their mental

individuality is unquestionable. When my voice awakened a train of old associations in the mind of my dog, he must have retained his mental individuality, although every atom of his brain had probably undergone change more than once during the interval of five years. This dog might have brought forward the argument lately advanced to crush all evolutionists, and said, 'I abide amid all mental moods and all material changes.'" (Vol. i. p. 63.)

Homo. No doubt, my Lord, Mr. Darwin's dog was the same dog he had been five years before, but, unquestionably, the dog did not possess that consciousness of his own mental individuality that would have enabled him either to reflect on it, or to affirm it. Mr. Darwin puts the words, "I abide amid all mental moods and all material changes," in his dog's mouth; but he cannot suppose either this thought, or this consciousness, to have existed in the dog's mind.

Lord C. It thus appears, Mr. Darwin, that you cannot prove any of the inferior animals to be possessed of the high faculties in question—*Self-consciousness, Abstraction, General Ideas,* or *Individuality.* When apes, and dogs, and horses become capable of *abstraction,* and can form *general ideas,* they will be able to use their powers of reason and imagination to better purpose than at present.

Darwin. The next point, my Lord, is "*The sense of beauty.* This sense has been declared to be peculiar to man. But when we behold male birds elaborately displaying their plumes and splendid colours before the females, while other birds, not thus decorated, make no such display, it is impossible to doubt that the females admire the beauty of their male partners." (Vol. i. p. 63.)

Homo. I willingly grant, my Lord, that the beauty of birds is a source of enjoyment to them, but this is quite a different thing from their having such a sense of beauty as man possesses. A bird can admire only itself, or others of its own species. Its sense of beauty has a very narrow range, though, within that range, it serves an evident and necessary purpose. But is any bird conscious of the beauty of flowers? Can a peacock, or a peahen, admire, or be taught to admire, a lily or a rose? Mr. Darwin himself says, "Obviously no animal would be capable of admiring such scenes as the heavens at night, a beautiful landscape, or refined music." "Such high tastes," he adds, "are not enjoyed by barbarians or uneducated persons." But barbarians and uneducated persons may easily be so cultured as to have these high tastes developed in them. This is more than can be said of any animal. In animals, the sense of beauty is but a confined and narrow instinct, which remains the same age after age; in man it is a high and complex faculty, which may be cultured and improved, and transmitted onwards, purified and refined, from generation to generation.

Lord C. I think, Mr. Darwin, you must admit that the sense of beauty which certain animals possess is a mere unimproveable instinct, operating within a very narrow range, and incapable of extension beyond that range; while, in man, this sense may be so trained as to become one of the loftiest faculties of his nature. Man can speak not only of a beautiful bird, or a beautiful flower, or a beautiful landscape, but of a beautiful poem, a beautiful chain of reasoning, the beautiful machinery of nature, and so on. I think you must wait till you find some animal going beyond itself and its own species, in its admiration of beauty, before you compare its sense of beauty with that possessed by man. What is the next point?

Darwin. "*Belief in God,*" my Lord; "*Religion.* There

is no evidence that man was aboriginally endowed with the ennobling belief in the existence of an Omnipotent God. On the contrary, there is ample evidence derived, not from hasty travellers, but from men who have long resided with savages, that numerous races have existed, and still exist, who have no idea of one or more gods, and who have no words in their languages to express such an idea. This question is, of course, wholly distinct from that higher one, whether there exists a creator and ruler of the universe; and this has been answered in the affirmative by the highest intellects that have ever lived." (Vol. i. p. 65.)

Homo. In what Mr. Darwin has just said, my Lord, he sets aside the Bible as having any claim whatever to be regarded as, in any sense, a revelation from God. Yet, if the highest intellects that ever lived have affirmed the existence of God, the highest intellects that have had the opportunity of investigating the question have affirmed the Bible to be his Word. We are not, however, going to discuss this question. But I wish to remark that, whether or not the Bible contain a revelation from God, even Mr. Darwin, I presume, will admit that it contains much true history. Now, in the early records of the Jews, we see a people who, unquestionably, at a very remote period, were " endowed with the ennobling belief in the existence of an Omnipotent God," casting this belief aside, and falling under the influence of the impure superstitions of the nations that surrounded them. It is well known, moreover, that, with a pure and elevating theism in their most ancient sacred books, the Hindoos rank among the most debased idolaters in the world. We see also, in our own country, that with this "ennobling belief" in the Divine existence within their reach, multitudes practically disregard and reject it. I make these remarks, my Lord, to show that, if there be races of men so degraded that they have no knowledge of God, their ignorance arises, far more probably, from their remote ancestors having lost this knowledge, than from man having been originally destitute of it. I beg to say, further, that when Mr. Darwin affirms there is no evidence that man originally possessed this belief, he is, as usual, taking for granted what he ought first to prove.

Lord C. There can be no doubt that many of the highest intellects that adorn our country would differ most decidedly from Mr. Darwin in his opinion on this question. But is it necessary for us to debate it?

Homo. Mr. Darwin, my Lord, does not debate it. He satisfies himself with dogmatically settling it in favour of his own side of the argument. Disbelieving, if not the existence of God, yet the intervention of God in human affairs, and maintaining that man is descended from an ape, he believes also, of course, that when man emerged from ape he was a savage. "The Creator and Ruler of the universe, whose existence has been affirmed by the highest intellects that ever lived," has never thought fit, according to Mr. Darwin, to reveal himself to the only creature on this earth capable, in some measure, of comprehending Him. Man has, all unaided and uncared for by the "Omnipotent God," struggled by his own efforts into the light and knowledge he now possesses. It is, moreover, altogether uncertain that the light which man possesses on "God" and "religion" is true light, or that his knowledge on these subjects is based on reality. Such is the conclusion to which Darwinism points us, my Lord!

Darwin. Allow me, my Lord, to state how it appears to me that religion has come to exist among men.

Lord C. By all means, Mr. Darwin; let us have your views on this point.

Darwin. "If," my Lord, "we include under the term 'religion' the belief in unseen or spiritual agencies ... this belief seems to be almost universal with the less civilized races. Nor is it difficult to comprehend how it arose. As soon as the important faculties of the imagination, wonder, and curiosity, together with some power of reasoning, had become partially developed, man would naturally have craved to understand what was passing around him, and have vaguely speculated on his own existence.... It is probable that dreams may have first given rise to the notion of spirits; for savages do not readily distinguish between subjective and objective impressions. When a savage dreams, the figures which appear before him are believed to have come from a distance and to stand over him; or 'the soul of the dreamer goes out on its travels, and comes home with a remembrance of what it has seen.' But, until the above-named faculties of imagination, curiosity, reason, &c., had been fairly well developed in the mind of man, his dreams would not have led him to believe in spirits any more than in the case of a dog.... The belief in spiritual agencies would easily pass into the belief in the existence of one or more gods. For savages would naturally attribute to spirits the same passions, the same love of vengeance or simplest form of justice, and the same affections which they themselves experienced." (Vol. i. pp. 65-67.)

Homo. Let us suppose, my Lord, for the sake of argument, that such religion as savages possess arose among them in the way which Mr. Darwin suggests, their dreams having had much to do with it. Will he now explain how it has happened that the dreams of dogs and horses—for he tells us that they also dream—have not resulted in their having some kind of religion? For, be it remembered, my Lord, that Mr. Darwin is now endeavouring to prove that the fact of man being capable of religion does not separate him by an impassable gulf from the lower animals. Is there evidence, then, that any of the lower animals are finding their way across the gulf, by this bridge of dreams?

Lord C. The point at present in debate, Mr. Darwin, is not how religion at first originated among savages, but whether the fact of man's capacity for religion does not show him to be possessed of a nature in which the lower animals do not share. The observations you have just made do not bear on this point. They show, however, that a belief in the supernatural is present in savages, which is more than can be said of dogs and horses. They, certainly, neither believe in the supernatural, nor are capable of such belief. Hence, religion is with them an impossibility.

Homo. Mr. Darwin, my Lord, has told us of one ape taking a first step in the formation of language, and of another taking a first step in architecture; can he find, or even imagine, one taking a first step in religion?

Darwin. "The tendency in savages," my Lord, "to imagine that natural objects and agencies are animated by spiritual or living essences, is perhaps illustrated by a little fact which I once noticed: My dog, a full grown and very sensible animal, was lying on the lawn during a hot and still day; but at a little distance a slight breeze occasionally moved an open parasol, which would have been wholly disregarded by the dog had any one stood near it. As it was, every time that the parasol slightly moved, the dog growled fiercely and barked. He must, I think, have reasoned to himself in a rapid and unconscious manner, that movement, without any apparent cause, indicated the presence of some strange living agent, and no stranger had a right to be on his territory." (Vol. i. p. 67.)

Lord C. The fact you mention, Mr. Darwin, though interesting, does not bear on the question before us. If you could show that he reasoned himself into a belief of the supernatural, it would be a case in point. But why should you suppose that your dog "reasoned" on this occasion? Might he not simply have felt as if the parasol itself, moving without any apparent cause, were some "strange living agent?"

Homo. Will your Lordship allow me to quote here a passage from an able review of Mr. Darwin's book, which recently appeared in *The Times*, and which bears on the point now before us:— "The nearest approach to reasoning which Mr. Darwin can adduce is furnished in two analogous stories respecting dogs. 'Mr. Colquhoun winged two wild ducks, which fell on the opposite side of a stream; his retriever tried to bring over both at once, but could not succeed; she then, though previously never known to ruffle a feather, deliberately killed one, brought over the other, and returned for the dead bird.' The case is certainly remarkable; but it appears to us a very hasty conclusion that the act was rational. The retriever possesses the instinct of not permitting a bird to escape as well as the instinct of not injuring it, and her act would seem simply an instance of one instinct overpowering another. This interpretation is strongly confirmed by the other story. In that case two partridges were shot, one being killed, the other wounded. The latter ran away, and was caught by the retriever, who, on her return, came across the dead bird; 'she stopped, evidently greatly puzzled, and after one or two trials, finding she could not take it up without permitting the escape of the winged bird, she considered a moment, and then deliberately murdered it by giving it a severe crunch, and afterwards brought away both together. This was the only known instance of her ever having wilfully injured any game.' 'Here,' says Mr. Darwin, 'we have reason, though not quite perfect, for the retriever might have brought the wounded bird first, and then returned for the dead one, as in the case of the two wild ducks.' Precisely so; if she had really reasoned she would not have killed the duck. But two instinctive impulses were working in her—one impelling her to bring both birds, the other impelling her not to let either bird escape; and, not being able to reconcile the two by means of reason, the latter instinct overpowered her habit of not injuring the game. It is not by such instances that the result of a wide induction respecting the difference between the faculties of men and brutes can be overthrown. We should have been, indeed, in no way surprised if Mr. Darwin had been able to adduce cases far more difficult of explanation. Nothing is better recognized than that inferior faculties, when acting alone, acquire a perfection of development which enables them in many cases to act even more efficiently than higher faculties. A blind man will perceive by the mere sense of touch that which the philosopher could only observe by the aid of a microscope; and a dog, by his acute sense of smell, will surpass the utmost exertions of human sagacity in tracking his prey. Consequently, even if it could be shown that animals perform certain actions which men could only perform by the aid of reason, it would by no means necessarily follow that animals perform them by its aid. It would be perfectly conceivable that their power was derived from the development of a lower and diverse faculty to an extent of which men have on experience. Such a consideration is alone enough to show that the question needs to be treated with infinitely more care and research than Mr. Darwin has thought worth while to bestow upon it."

Darwin. "I have to say yet farther," my Lord, "on this subject, that the feeling of religious devotion is a highly complex one, consisting of love, complete submission to an exalted and mysterious superior, a strong sense of dependence, fear, reverence, gratitude, hope for the future, and perhaps other elements. No being could experience so complex an emotion, until advanced in his intellectual and moral faculties to at least a moderately high level. Nevertheless, we see some distinct approach to this state of mind in the deep love of a dog for his master, associated with complete submission, some fear, and perhaps other feelings. The behaviour of a dog, when returning to his master after an absence, and, as I may add, of a monkey to his beloved keeper, is widely different from that towards their fellows. In the latter case the transports of joy appear to be somewhat less, and the sense of equality is shown in every action. Professor Braubach goes so far as to maintain that a dog looks on his master as on a god." (Vol. i. p. 68.)

Homo. Which would imply, my Lord, that the dog has formed the idea of a god. If Mr. Darwin could show this to be the case, it would afford some help to his argument. But though he quotes this professor's language, and evidently would gladly endorse it if he could, he does not venture on the absurdity. Professor Braubach should bring out a dog's catechism, in which, in reply to the question, "Who made you?" the creature should be taught to reply, "My master!"

Lord C. You do not, Mr. Darwin, mention regard for truth, purity, and rectitude, as mingling in "the highly complex feeling of religious devotion," of which you speak. Yet, would not these elements also have a place in it?

Homo. In page 182, my Lord, Mr. Darwin speaks of "the highest form of religion—the grand idea of God hating sin and loving righteousness." For this idea he is of course indebted to the book he so persistently ignores in discussing this question. I presume he omitted this idea in the description he has just given of religious devotion, because he intended to exhibit the dog as showing "some distant approach" to a religious state of mind, and knew that he would search in vain, in any dog, for the faintest shadow of hatred to sin and love to righteousness.

Lord C. To bring in this idea here would certainly encumber his argument. Nevertheless, it must be brought in, if the whole case is to be before us. Do you object, Homo, to what Mr. Darwin has just said regarding the dog—his "deep love for his master, associated with complete submission, some fear, and perhaps other feelings?"

Homo. By no means, my Lord; the dog is a most noble animal, and Mr. Darwin, I think, has spoken quite correctly regarding him. But he is nothing more than an animal endowed with instincts that lead him to attach himself to man. He acts from instinctive impulses, and neither reflects nor reasons on his conduct. I cannot see that a dog has any end in view in attaching himself to man, or that he knows why he does so. I need not say to your Lordship that the feeling of religious devotion, even as Mr. Darwin has described it, can arise only from the exercise of reason. Mr. Darwin himself indeed allows this, for he tells us that "no being could experience so complex an emotion until advanced in his intellectual and moral faculties to at least a moderately high level." While, in the feelings of a dog towards his master, then, we see merely the working of instinct; in the feeling of religious devotion in man, the loftiest reason comes into play. If a dog's feelings may thus, in the case before us, be compared to a man's, it is not because they proceed from the working of the same, or even of similar faculties. The instinct, or—if you will—the reason of a dog is no more identical with the reason of a man than a shadow is identical with the substance from which it is thrown.

Lord C. You have said nothing, Homo, on the grand idea of hatred to sin and love to righteousness, which we proposed to bring into the discussion of this point.

Homo. I beg your Lordship's pardon for the omission. Of course a dog, or any animal whatever, is utterly incapable either of understanding or feeling the power of this grand idea. A dog's attachment to his master is altogether irrespective of either sin or righteousness. He will be as much attached to Bill Sikes, if he be his master, as to William Wilberforce. As to a dog approaching to anything like a conception, or a consciousness of a pure and righteous God, such a thing should not even be named; nor will it be unless by men who have a stronger tendency downward towards communion with the brute creation, than up towards God.

Lord C. Mr. Darwin, I presume, advances nothing more than what has come before us to prove that the capacity of man for religion does not separate him by " an impassable barrier from all the lower animals."

Homo. Nothing more that I am aware of, my Lord. His second chapter concludes with this subject. In his third chapter he discusses the moral sense.

Lord C. We shall now hear what he has to say regarding it.

Darwin. " I fully subscribe," my Lord, " to the judgment

of those writers who maintain that, of all the differences between man and the lower animals, the moral sense or conscience is by far the most important. This sense, as Mackintosh remarks, 'has a rightful supremacy over every other principle of human action;' it is summed up in that short but imperious word *ought*, so full of high significance. It is the most noble of all the attributes of man, leading him without a moment's hesitation to risk his life for that of a fellow creature; or, after due deliberation, impelled simply by the deep feeling of right or duty, to sacrifice it in some great cause. Immanuel Kant exclaims, 'Duty! wondrous thought, that workest neither by fond insinuation, flattery, nor by any threat, but merely by holding up thy naked "law in the soul," and so extorting for thyself always reverence, if not always obedience; before whom all appetites are dumb, however secretly they rebel; whence thy original?'" (Vol. i. pp. 70, 71.)

Lord C. I heartily assent to your quotations from Mackintosh and Kant, and also to your own remark that the moral sense "is summed up in the short but imperious word *ought;*" but do you find anything answering to the moral sense or conscience in the lower animals?

Darwin. "The following proposition," my Lord, "seems to me in a high degree probable, namely, that any animal whatever, endowed with well-marked social instincts, would inevitably acquire a moral sense or conscience, as soon as its intellectual powers had become as well developed, or nearly as well developed, as in man." (Vol. i. pp. 71, 72.)

Lord C. Cannot you give us facts, Mr. Darwin, instead merely of a proposition which seems to you in a high degree probable? Your hypothesis should be sustained on something more substantial than probabilities — probabilities, moreover, which may seem such only to yourself.

Homo. Your Lordship doubtless perceives that, in order to find these probabilities, Mr. Darwin takes it for granted that the intellectual powers of an animal possessing social instincts may become " as well developed," or nearly as well developed, "as they are in man." He thus seems unable to take a single step towards proving his hypothesis without taking it for granted.

Lord C. I understand you then to admit, Mr. Darwin, that a moral sense or conscience is impossible unless in a creature whose intellectual powers are at least nearly as well developed as man's.

Darwin. What I say, my Lord, clearly implies this.

Lord C. We are thrown back, then, on your previous argument, for you have certainly not proved that any animal possesses intellectual powers capable of being developed into anything approaching to equality with those of man.

Homo. Your Lordship is perfectly correct. Mr. Darwin has clearly put himself out of court on this question by admitting—what, indeed, he cannot help admitting—that a moral sense is impossible without human reason. But it may help to bring this case to a more satisfactory settlement if your Lordship will listen while Mr. Darwin states the process by which he supposes animals may acquire a moral sense, and while he mentions his views regarding the nature of the moral sense.

Lord C. I am quite ready to hear what Mr. Darwin has to say on these points.

Darwin. What I have to say, my Lord, is this, "Any animal whatever, endowed with well-marked social instincts, would inevitably acquire a moral sense or conscience, as soon as its intellectual powers had become as well developed, or nearly as well developed, as in man.

For, *Firstly*, the social instincts lead an animal to take pleasure in the society of its fellows, to feel a certain amount of sympathy with them, and to perform various services for them. The services may be of a definite and evidently instinctive nature; or there may be only a wish and readiness, as with most of the higher social animals, to aid their fellows in certain general ways. But these feelings and services are by no means extended to all the individuals of the same species, only to those of the same association. *Secondly*, as soon as the mental faculties had become highly developed, images of all past actions and motives would be incessantly passing through the brain of each individual; and that feeling of dissatisfaction which invariably results, as we shall hereafter see, from an unsatisfied instinct, would arise, as often as it was perceived that the enduring and always present social instinct had yielded to some other instinct, at the time stronger, but neither enduring in its nature, nor leaving behind it a very vivid impression. It is clear that many instinctive desires, such as that of hunger, are in their nature of short duration; and after being satisfied are not readily or vividly recalled. *Thirdly*, after the power of language had been acquired, and the wishes of the members of the same community could be distinctly expressed, the common opinion, how each member ought to act for the public good, would naturally become to a large extent the guide to action. But the social instincts would still give the impulse to act for the good of the community, this impulse being strengthened, directed, and sometimes even deflected by public opinion, the power of which rests, as we shall presently see, on instinctive sympathy. *Lastly*, habit in the individual would ultimately play a very important part in guiding the conduct of each member; for the social instincts and impulses, like all other instincts, would be greatly strengthened by habit, as would obedience to the wishes and judgment of the community." (Vol. I. pp. 71, 73.)

Lord C. And in this way you imagine that from irrational and irresponsible brutes were developed rational, thoughtful, and responsible men. But all this is mere supposition, without even a tittle of evidence to sustain it. It would be more to the purpose if you could refer us to any species of animals which is passing through the process you describe. Can you point to any instance, among the lower animals, in which a moral sense or conscience is now being developed?

Homo. Mr. Darwin cannot do that, my Lord. "The common rat," to which he has referred as having had "all its faculties habitually exercised" through man, does not serve him here; yet, I believe it is a social animal. No ape, nor monkey of any kind, gives the least sign of advancement in this pathway to humanity, which Mr. Darwin has sketched for them. Even the dog, though, as Professor Braubach maintains, he is so advanced in intellect that "he looks on his master as on a god," refuses his help on this subject. In vain would Mr. Darwin lecture him on conscience and the moral sense. All that the poor brute could do would be to look interested and wag his tail, pleased at the notice taken of him, and perhaps wondering what it meant—for, as Mr. Darwin tells us, "all animals feel wonder"—but not one step nearer to the possession of a conscience or moral sense would he advance. Let Mr. Darwin try the experiment even with that dog of his which "growled fiercely and barked" every time that the open parasol was slightly moved by the wind, "reasoning to himself, in a rapid and unconscious manner, that movement, without any apparent cause, indicated the presence of some strange living agent, who had no right to be on his territory," thus arriving almost at a conception of the supernatural—let Mr. Darwin, I say, try the experiment even with this "very sensible animal," and he will find it vain."

Darwin. "It may be wel first to premise," my Lord, "that I do not wish to maintain that any strictly social animal, if its intellectual faculties were to become as active and as highly developed as in man, would acquire exactly the same moral sense as ours. In the same manner as various animals have some sense of beauty, though they admire widely different objects, so they might have a sense of right and wrong, though led by it to follow widely different lines of conduct. If, for instance, to take an extreme case, men were reared under precisely the same conditions as hive-bees, there can hardly be a doubt that our unmarried females would, like the worker-bees, think it a sacred duty to kill their brothers, and mothers would strive to kill their fertile daughters, and no one would think of interfering. Nevertheless, the bee, or any other social animal, would, in our supposed case, gain, as it appears to me, some feeling of right or wrong, or conscience. For each individual would have an inward sense of possessing certain stronger or more enduring instincts, and others less strong or enduring, so that there would often be a struggle, which impulse should be followed, and satisfaction or dissatisfaction would be felt, as past impressions were compared during their incessant passage through the mind. In this case an inward monitor would tell the animal that it would have been better to have followed the one impulse rather than the other." (Vol. i. p. 73.)

Lord C. You seem now, Mr. Darwin, to take a different

view of morality from what you did at the outset. You have but just spoken of conscience as "the most noble of all the attributes of man, leading him, without a moment's hesitation, to risk his life for that of a fellow creature." Now you suppose it possible that sisters might be impelled by conscience to murder their brothers, and mothers their daughters!

Darwin. This doubtless is "an extreme case," my Lord, but, if men were reared under precisely the same conditions as hive-bees, there can hardly be a doubt that the members of the same family would think it a sacred duty to kill one another, and that no one would think of interfering.

Lord C. You reason in a most extraordinary manner, Mr. Darwin. You suppose an impossible case, and you expound to us a system of morals founded on this impossible case, which morals are not morals at all, but acts arising from instinctive impulses, and followed by different feelings as the animal compares the impressions that pass through its mind one with another. But all this is entirely imaginary.

Homo. I call it reasoning with the imagination, my Lord, an operation which Mr. Darwin performs with great facility. But, in his supposed case, the development goes the wrong way, for it makes man develop into a bee, instead of making the bee develop into a man. Mr. Darwin might suppose other cases quite as probable as the one before us. He might suppose man reared under precisely the same conditions as rooks, or jackdaws, or starlings; or as dogs, horses, sheep, or rabbits—all of which animals he goes on to speak of as social in their habits—and he might exhibit to us a new system of morals as springing from each case. We should have thus rook-morality, and rabbit-morality, and horse and dog-morality, &c., as well as bee-morality and man-morality.

Lord C. Such supposed cases do not throw one spark of light on the question before us—Can any animal whatever acquire a moral sense or conscience?

Homo. Very true, my Lord; but they illustrate Mr. Darwin's views on morals. There is another passage in his work bearing on this subject, to which I must beg your Lordship's attention. At page 168, treating of "Natural Selection as affecting Civilized Nations," he says, "With savages the weak in body or mind are soon eliminated, and those that survive commonly exhibit a vigorous state of health. We civilized men, on the other hand, do our utmost to check the process of elimination; we build asylums for the imbecile, the maimed, and the sick; we institute poor laws, and our medical men exert their utmost skill to save the life of every one to the last moment. There is reason to believe that vaccination has preserved thousands, who from a weak constitution would formerly have succumbed to small-pox. Thus the weak members of civilized societies propagate their kind. No one who has attended to the breeding of domestic animals will doubt that this must be highly injurious to the race of man. It is surprising how soon a want of care, or care wrongly directed, leads to the degeneration of a domestic race; but excepting in the case of man himself, hardly any one is so ignorant as to allow his worst animals to breed."

Lord C. Does Mr. Darwin mean to say then that, in building asylums for the imbecile, the maimed, the sick; instituting poor laws; enforcing vaccination—endeavouring thus to prolong the lives of our fellow-creatures—we are directing our care wrongly, and causing a degeneration of the race of man?

Homo. I have read what Mr. Darwin says, and must leave your Lordship to form your own judgment regarding it.

Lord C. Why, had it not been for vaccination, we ourselves might have fallen victims to small-pox!

Homo. Mr. Darwin might, most assuredly, my Lord. May I say that I heard it stated lately that Mr. Darwin had been prevented from attending to some public engagement by ill health? Probably that was not the first time he had suffered in this way. Now, had the process of elimination been adopted in his own case, his work on "The descent of man," might never have been written, and we should not now be engaged in these proceedings.

Lord C. I think, Homo, you are becoming a little too personal in making such a remark. It may be questioned, however, whether, even from a scientific point of view, it would be wise to disregard the weak and feeble, or have them put out of the way. Newton himself was born prematurely, and as an infant, was of extremely diminutive size. Intellectual energy and physical strength do not necessarily go together.

Darwin. My Lord, Homo ought in fairness to state what follows. I add that, "We could not check our sympathy, if so urged by hard reason, without deterioration in the noblest part of our nature. The surgeon may harden himself whilst performing an operation, for he knows that he is acting for the good of his patient; but if we were intentionally to neglect the weak and helpless, it could only be for a contingent benefit, with a certain and great present evil. Hence we must bear without complaining the undoubtedly bad effects of the weak surviving and propagating their kind." (Vol. i. pp. 168, 169.)

Homo. Would these passages from Mr. Darwin's work,

my Lord, be suitable for a lesson-book to be introduced into our National Schools? Would it help to educate the rising race in morals, were they led to consider the case in which it might be a sacred duty with sisters to kill their brothers? Would it also tend to strengthen their compassion for the maimed, the suffering, and the sick, were they taught that, though their care would be wrongly directed, if directed towards them, and would tend to the deterioration of the race, yet they could not check their feelings of sympathy towards them without deterioration in the noblest part of their nature? Would such lessons in morals, my Lord, given to the rising generation, tend to their advancement and elevation?

Lord C. I fear it would not be easy to induce any English constituency to elect Mr. Darwin to the School Board.

Homo. Especially, my Lord, if, in his address to the electors, he were to quote these passages as setting forth his views on conscience and morals. The common sense of Englishmen would revolt from them. Mr. Darwin, my Lord, has more faith in "Natural Selection," and in the process of "Elimination," by which the weak in body and mind are gradually killed off—he has more faith in these processes as tending to human advancement than he has in the "Omnipotent God," whom he tells us it is "ennobling" to believe in.

Lord C. Are you not rather hard on Mr. Darwin in saying so?

Homo. I think not, my Lord. The whole tendency of his book is to eliminate the Divine Being from among his works, and to set up Natural Selection in his place. According to Mr. Darwin, the "Omnipotent God" does nothing, except, perhaps, create at first. He then withdraws from the universe, and, for aught that appears, goes to sleep like the Brahma of the Hindoos. Meanwhile, Natural Selection, assisted by Sexual Selection and Evolution, steps in and does the work. We have thus to do, not with the "Omnipotent God," but with the inferior deities discovered by Mr. Darwin, of whose existence he tells us in his book. It is they alone who are to be our fear and our dread.

Darwin. I have said, my Lord, that we could not check the feelings of sympathy towards the weak and helpless without deterioration in the noblest part of our nature.

Homo. Very true, my Lord, he has said so; but what are our sympathies, according to him, but merely feelings which have arisen from the process of Natural Selection, and which, if we had been reared as hive-bees, would never have existed in us. And does he not plainly tell us our sympathies are wrongly directed, and tend to the degeneration of the race, when bestowed on the objects that most need them? It had thus been better for our race, on Mr. Darwin's principles, that we had had no such sympathies as Natural Selection has unfortunately given us.

Darwin. I have also spoken, my Lord, of "the grand idea of God hating sin and loving righteousness."

Homo. Very true, he has, my Lord; but then, on his hypothesis, righteousness is not a great, living, necessary reality, based on the nature of God, and therefore unchangeable and enduring as God himself; but a mere accidental and unstable quality, generated by the social instincts of brutes, and which might have been quite different from what it happens to be, and led to widely different, and even opposite lines of conduct, and yet been righteousness still. I do not see, for my part, how one can believe in an "Omnipotent God," the "Creator and Ruler of the universe," and in this God as "hating sin and loving righteousness," and yet fail to see that the moral sense and conscience, in such a creature as man, when rightly exercised, must have reference to God's will.

Lord C. Will Homo inform me if he has now anything farther to advance?

Homo. Your Lordship has now before you the whole of the particulars of the libel of which I complain. After the patient attention given to those particulars by your Lordship, I shall not attempt a review of the case. I leave it with your Lordship, satisfied that I shall be indemnified, so far as is in your Lordship's power, for the injury inflicted on me by the publication of the Defendant's book. I may observe, however, that Mr. Darwin's speculations are injurious also in this way—they lead others who are dissatisfied with them into speculations of their own quite as wild and visionary. Some scientific gentlemen are now actually engaged in trying to create life! Other men of science are not so daring in their experiments, but they are quite as audacious in their suggestions. They tell us that life may have been imported into this planet on a meteoric stone! I suppose, my Lord, that after some more time has been vainly expended in searching for the missing links of Evolution, we shall be hearing that the first human pair were charioted into our world on a shooting star!

Lord C. Speculations on the mystery of life are generally so absurd that they speedily refute themselves. It is indeed possible that germs of life may have been conveyed in meteoric stones, but that life in our world was thus originated can never be proved. Besides, such a supposition does not solve the mystery of life; it but removes it one step back, and renders it more than ever difficult for us to deal with. If life was not originated in our world, but merely imported into it, our naturalists would require to visit the world where it first appeared before they could be competent for dealing satisfactorily with the subject. Yet, though such speculations are unsatisfactory, probably, it will only be through speculation and experiment that the truth will be reached at last. The human mind seeks after unity in creation—tries to find some definite point from which all has sprung. My own belief is that the unity and starting-point of creation will be sought after in vain till they are sought for in God. To my mind, there is more light and wisdom in those grand old words of the Psalmist, "With Thee is the fountain of life"—"Thou sendest forth Thy Spirit, they are created: Thou renewest the face of the earth"—than there is in all such speculations of philosophers. I will deliver my judgment at our sitting to-morrow.

SIXTH DAY'S SITTING.

THE JUDGMENT OF LORD C.

Having carefully considered the evidence that has been adduced, and having also carefully examined Mr. Darwin's book, I can have no hesitation in saying that his hypothesis does not account for the existence of man. According to that hypothesis we are to believe that all the varied forms of animal life existing on this earth have been produced by the action of laws now in operation around us, from some one, or from a few, primary forms. We are to believe that, by minute variations of this form or forms—which variations went on accumulating, generation after generation, through a period of time incalculably long—one species of creature after another has been produced; that the larvæ of ascidians developed into fish; fish into amphibians; amphibians into reptiles and birds; these into mammals, including the Old World monkeys, through which the climax was at last reached in man.

Such hypotheses are not new. They are as old as the history of human thought. In ancient times men of speculative tendencies discussed the origin of the universe and of man; and development and evolution, in one form or another, were employed to account for what they saw around them. In more recent times Lamarck supposed species to have been produced by the operation on organized creatures of the conditions and circumstances in which they were placed—the giraffe, for example, as alluded to by Homo, acquiring its long neck, and other corresponding peculiarities of its frame, from having to stretch its body in order to feed on the lofty branches of trees; and monkeys, I presume, acquiring their powers of climbing by having to ascend still higher to find the fruit. So pass over Lord Monboddo's opinions on the origin of man. Mr. Darwin's own grandfather, Dr. Erasmus Darwin, is known to have entertained somewhat similar views. Mr. Darwin has advanced on these ideas by introducing Natural Selection as the primary modifying agent. Starting from the position of Malthus, with regard to man, Mr. Darwin maintains that many more living creatures are produced on this earth than can possibly survive. It is well known, moreover, that, by what may be called the law of variation, each living creature produced differs, to some extent, from every other of its kind. No two human beings are exactly alike, and these variations extend, not only to the features, but every separate member and portion of the frame. So it is with the lower animals. Mr. Darwin supposes that those individuals, in which the variations are of a favourable character, will be more vigorous, or, at least, more fit for the conditions in which they are placed; and that, consequently, in the struggle for existence with their own kind, with other animals, and with external circumstances, they will survive in greater numbers, and that, by the laws of inheritance, they will transmit their peculiarities to their offspring; and that thus the struggle for existence, and the survival of the fittest being continually renewed, by the gradual accumulation of favourable peculiarities, through numerous generations, separate and distinct species are eventually produced.

The lengthened time—3,000 years at least—during which cosmological speculations have been cherished, has given ample opportunity for testing them; and had the development hypothesis been based on fact, and supported by observation and experience, it must long, ere now, in some form or other, have found its way to the general belief of mankind. Within a much shorter period—300 years instead of 3,000—such theories as those of gravitation, the circulation of the blood, the influence of the moon on the tides, have established themselves in the convictions of all persons of intelligence. No views put forth on Evolution, however, have gained such acceptance, and the idea is entertained only by some men of speculative mind, through the operation of tendencies characteristic of the present age. These facts I take as, at least, *primâ facie* evidence that the basis of proof is not only insufficient, but unsatisfactory so far as it goes.

That Mr. Darwin's hypothesis rests on no stable basis is shown, moreover, by the fact that he has himself, oftener than once, shifted its supports. In his earlier works, Natural Selection was the all-sufficient power by which everything was accomplished. Through the wide field of organized existence, from its origin, myriads of ages ago, until now, Mr. Darwin could see no power in operation but that of Natural Selection. Not only were Divine wisdom and purpose unrecognized—except, indeed, that God was supposed to have at first "breathed life into a few forms or into one"—but all other laws and powers whatever were put in abeyance. Natural Selection was the one presiding Deity in the world of animated and organic existence.

Mr. Darwin now acknowledges himself to have been mistaken. "I probably attributed too much (he says) to the action of Natural Selection, or the survival of the fittest;" and he, therefore, now brings in "Sexual Selection," with "the nature and constitution of the organism itself," and also "unknown agencies," as playing an important part in the production of the changes for which he formerly maintained that Natural Selection alone was sufficient to account. Thus, as Mr. Darwin's knowledge of the world of animated nature increases, so does his consciousness of ignorance as to the powers and processes working in connection with it. He finds life to be a greater mystery than ever. After the researches of a lifetime, he finds it obstinately refusing to reveal itself to him, and ever retreating farther and farther from his gaze. And thus he comes to learn, what all his predecessors have learned, and what, most probably, his contemporaries also will have to learn— that there are powers and agencies at work in connection with life which baffle the keenest pursuit, and that there is something in "the nature and constitution" of every living creature which we cannot comprehend. The acknowledged mystery which thus veils life, in its nature and origin, from human research, should induce modesty in those whose studies lead them to consider it, and restrain them from the formation of rash and vain hypotheses.

Taking Mr. Darwin's hypothesis, however, as it is now presented to us, it is confessedly destitute of anything like proof. Professor Huxley, with assuredly no bias against it, yet admits that he can point to no "group of animals, having all the characters exhibited by species in nature, that has ever been originated by Selection, whether natural or artificial;" and Mr. Darwin himself can give us no facts that prove even the possibility of the evolution for which he contends. History and the experience of living men are equally appealed to in vain for help on this subject. Yet, if this process of "Selection" be one which, as Mr. Darwin contends, is ever going on in nature, it might reasonably be expected that some unmistakeable phenomena in connection with it would, some time or other, have forced themselves on the observation of mankind. It is not pretended, however, that anything like this has ever occurred, and when this consideration is adduced as tending to disprove the hypothesis, refuge is always sought from it in the enormous periods of time requisite for the formation of new species.

There is one consideration which, so far as I am aware, has not been urged in connection with this branch of the argument. Why are enormous periods of time required for the production of new species, but that there may be numerous successive generations, each of which may be supposed to have advanced on its predecessors? Now it is clear that, in the case of numerous animals, the period of time required for this purpose would be much less than in the case of man. We may suppose that three generations of men are produced in a century. This would give ninety generations in 3,000 years, which may be regarded as the historic period in connection with this subject. But, within the same period, we must have had not less than 3,000 generations of those numerous species of creatures which produce a fresh progeny every year, or even oftener than that. There have thus been 3,000 successive generations of many of the lower animals within a period during which men may have been expected to observe and record any remarkable changes occurring among them. What, then, is the sum of the changes which Mr. Darwin is able to point to within the historic period as tending to prove his hypothesis? It amounts absolutely to nothing! Yet Mr. Darwin tells us that Natural Selection is a kind of god that never slumbers nor sleeps; that scrutinizes everything; is ever selecting what is useful and profitable, in animal existence, and preserving it, that it may be transmitted to future generations; and that, through these accumulated and inherited useful variations in animal life, new species are developed.

Take the case, then, of any species of animal which produces young within a year of its birth. We have references in the writings of ancient naturalists to many of them. We have pictures of them on ancient monuments. We find skeletons of them in ancient tombs, and in mounds and caves. There are thus many animals living now which can be compared with their progenitors of the 3,000th generation back. Can Mr. Darwin show, then, in the case of any one of them, that, by successive variations accumulated during 3,000 generations, it has sensibly advanced towards some higher form? Can he show that 3,000 generations have, in any instance, done aught towards proving the truth of his hypothesis? It appears that he cannot point to a single such case as yielding him support. 3,000 generations have done literally nothing for his hypothesis. If so, neither would 30,000, nor 300,000; for, as Homo truly remarked, if you multiply nothing by a million, it will be nothing still.

Taking this view of the historical period, such evidence as it affords does not assist Mr. Darwin's hypothesis. But what of experiments made by naturalists—Natural Selection aided by human reason? Men have long been engaged in the breeding of cattle. We have records of human skill and ingenuity in this department during a longer period than 3,000 years. We know, moreover, that domestic animals, and animals dependant on man, can easily be modified. Important modifications have been produced even within the present century. But has anything been accomplished towards the production of a new species? Professor Huxley, somewhat reluctantly it would appear, answers "No." Even by crossing different species, nothing has been effected. The curse of sterility rests on all creatures produced beyond the bounds set by Nature. They are unable to propagate their kind. Thus, so far as observation and experiment go, they are both against Mr. Darwin.

The appeal to geology is equally vain. Though, if Mr. Darwin's hypothesis be true, there must have been a series of forms graduating from some lower form, not only up to man, but up to every kind of creature at present living on the earth, no one of these series of forms can be found; nor even such a portion of one of them as to afford ground for belief that the series was a reality.

If a few successive links in some one of these innumerable chains of descent could be produced, they would speak, so far, convincingly on behalf of Mr. Darwin's hypothesis. But, of the myriads of successive links, in myriads of chains of animal descent which must have existed if this hypothesis be true, not even two links can be produced which so fit as to show that they once were joined. I am aware that Professor Huxley, in a lecture delivered by him on "The Pedigree of the Horse," stated that the rocks show transitional forms, but he would entirely fail in attempting to prove that the horse is *descended* from any form different from itself.

There are thus absolutely no facts either in the records of geology, or in the history of the past, or in the experience of the present, that can be referred to as proving evolution, or the development of one species from another by selection of any kind whatever. Mr. Darwin himself is so conscious of this that the whole of the evidence he adduces in proof of his hypothesis is derived from those points of similarity that exist between the bodily structure of man and that of the lower animals. It appears to me that his argument, founded on the existence of those resemblances, has been fairly and satisfactorily answered. As man possesses an animal nature, and has to live on this earth, it is not strange that his bodily frame should be constructed after the model of other animals.

As to Mr. Darwin's argument from the resemblances between the embryos of man and those of the lower animals, it is sufficient to reply to it that, as there are resemblances in their bodily structures when mature, there must necessarily be resemblances in them when in process of development. We have the authority of Professor Owen for affirming that "the embryo" of man "does not pass through the lower forms of animals," and in the drawing which Mr. Darwin produces to show the similarity between the embryos of man and dog, the differences are so apparent as to make one wonder how he could have imagined that such an exhibition would help his argument.

He points us, moreover, to the existence of what he calls "rudimentary structures" in the human body—structures which are found fully developed only in some of the lower animals; and he attributes the occasional existence of such structures in man to a tendency in him to "revert" to the type of some ancient progenitor. The instances which he adduces, however, are so trivial and uncertain that I am amazed they could aid in justifying, even to his own mind, the astounding inference that the ape is father to the man. They are sufficiently accounted for, to my mind, by a reference to the unity of conception and plan traceable among the whole of the mammalia, and to the fact that the variations of structure that occur in the human body are almost innumerable. Mr. Darwin has told us of "558 muscular variations in thirty-six subjects," and of "a single body presenting the extraordinary number of twenty-five distinct abnormalities." If *all* these variations and abnormalities were in the direction of the monkey, and the body of man was thus manifesting a constant tendency toward the monkey type, there would be some show of reason for seeking its origin in that quarter; but when it is only *occasionally*—I may say, *rarely*—that the variations in question glance towards the simian tribe, and when it is but a very few out of the large number of these variations that do so, to argue from so trivial a circumstance that man is descended from the ape, is an abuse both of logic and common sense.

Besides, if a few of those variations look towards the ape, in what direction do the many look? It is not pretended that they also point us downward. Are they pre-intimations, then, of some higher form yet to be developed from man? In writing regarding those cases which he calls "reversions," Mr. Darwin should have kept in mind his own words, "With respect to the causes of variability, we are, in all cases, very ignorant." But he invariably forgets those words when, now and then, he meets with some variation which he imagines points in the direction of the brute. Then, he knows the cause perfectly! It lies in the fact that we are descended from apes! Mr. Darwin should be more consistent. I think, therefore, that, until we know more about those "causes of variability," of which, as he tells us, "we are in all cases very ignorant," or until we have some more reliable evidence of the truth of his hypothesis, we must, in all fairness, set down those instances which he quotes as proving our descent from the lower animals, as instances, not of reversion, but of simple variation.

It will not be necessary for me to refer at any length to

the changes, or series of changes, through which Mr. Darwin supposes the "ape-like progenitors of man" to have entered on this fatherly relation. The account he gives of the matter certainly does not lack romance, for, while "some ancient member in the great series of the Primates" becomes strangely plastic, Nature also becomes plastic, and in such a way as to assist in the transformation. There is a change in this creature's "manner of procuring subsistence, or a change in the conditions of its native country." Perhaps the climate changes; it blows cold instead of hot; or it grows fewer trees; or such fruits as are produced are not tempting enough to the creature's taste. However this may be, it becomes convenient for the creature to "live somewhat less on trees and more on the ground," and hence to "become either more strictly quadrupedal or bipedal." One might suppose that the former direction, as being the easier of the two, would be chosen, in which case it would simply revert to a former type, its ancestors having been quadrupeds; but somehow it takes the bipedal direction, and having ceased to climb trees, begins to climb up towards man. Everything conspires to help its progress. As the conditions of its native country have changes, its bodily structure changes to correspond with them. Before this creature, or rather, I should say, its progeny, can attain to intelligent and civilized manhood, they must pass through the savage state. They must therefore become able to "manufacture weapons," to "hurl stones and spears with a true aim," "to defend themselves with stones or clubs, to attack their prey, or otherwise obtain food." It will therefore be "advantageous" to them "to become more and more erect or bipedal." "Both arms and the whole upper part of the body should be free." They "must, for this end, stand firmly on their feet." These creatures, therefore, "assume the erect attitude!" Their feet are "rendered flat, and the great toe peculiarly modified, though this has entailed the loss of the power of prehension." The hands, now used less for such rough work as climbing trees, acquire a human delicateness of touch. "The pelvis" is "made broader, the spine peculiarly curved, and the head fixed in an altered position. The brain increases in size, and rational intellect is developed. They become "divested of hair for ornamental purposes," and at length the tail—now a rather inconvenient appendage of the brute—is somehow got rid of, leaving only a "few basal and tapering segments," which "become completely embedded within the body." Thus, from the ape, by a series of "insensible" gradations, there rises, at length, the man! Such, at least, expressed in very nearly his own words, is Mr. Darwin's avowed belief.

It would be humiliating, though curious, were Mr. Darwin's hypothesis true, to reflect on the strange and merely animal contingencies on which the existence of the human race has depended. If the bodily structure of some ancient member of the Primates had not been wonderfully plastic;—if he had not wooed and won for himself a mate of like plastic frame; if their posterity had not inherited their plastic qualities; if there had not been a change in their manner of procuring subsistence, or in the conditions of their native country; if they had not thus become somewhat less arboreal in their habits; if they had not then begun to change in a bipedal, and not in a quadrupedal direction; if any one of these contingencies had not occurred, the human race had never existed; there would still have been the hairy quadruped, with tail and pointed ears, living on the trees of African forests, but man, "the wonder and glory of the universe," had not come forth to subdue the world and fill it with monuments of his art and skill. There would have been no naturalist devoting a life-time to the study of the instincts, and habits, and anatomy of the lower animals; fancying he has discovered that he himself, instead of having a celestial origin, is one in nature with those lower animals, and sprung from the same primal stock: hence, searching among extinct brute species for his pedigree; persuading himself, and trying to persuade others, that he has found it; and then writing down the links of which he imagines the chain of his descent to be composed, though he is unable to find a fossil skeleton, or even a fossil bone, to prove that any one of those links is a reality!

Those who accept Mr. Darwin's account of the descent of man must accept along with it not a little that is, if possible, even more incredible. For example, while a certain monkey race has, by a series of insensible gradations, occurring during a period of enormous length, developed into man, other monkey races, during a yet longer period, have remained monkeys, making no progress whatever! Mr. Darwin, I presume, would maintain that at least half a million of years have passed since man emerged into humanity from the last of his ape-like progenitors. How far remote, then, must be the time when the ape from which man has descended, branched away from the stem of the Old World monkeys! But during this period—so long that, to us, it is practically an eternity—Old World monkeys have remained Old World monkeys, with the solitary exception of that wonderful member of the ancient series of the Primates, with his plastic frame, of which Mr. Darwin catches " an obscure glance" through the dim vista of ages.

In accepting Mr. Darwin's hypothesis then, we must believe that, since this creature, millions upon millions of ages ago, began its journey from monkeyhood to humanity, there have been none of his relatives either among the Old World monkeys or the New World monkeys that have had the capacity or the ambition to imitate his example; or that, if any there were, they perished in the attempt! Perhaps, as in the case of Mr. Darwin's ape, the progeny destroyed the parents, in other cases the parents may have destroyed the progeny. At all events, while the stem of Old World monkeys and the stem of New World monkeys survives and flourishes to the present day, no branch proceeding from either of them has been so favoured, except the branch that has blossomed into man. Such being the case, then, Old World monkeys and New World monkeys having, on Mr. Darwin's own showing, continued to be Old World and New World monkeys for millions upon millions of ages, in spite of the constant watchfulness and incessant and powerful working of Natural Selection—Mr. Darwin's god that never slumbers nor sleeps—can it be believed that this ancient member of the Primates ever existed to secede from their society and cross the gulf which now separates all of them from man? I should hope, for the credit of our common rationality, that there are but few of "the younger and rising naturalists" who possess credulity enough to accept such a belief.*

If Mr. Darwin thus fails on the field of Natural History,

---

* The writer has just had his attention drawn to the following notice in *The Academy*, of September 1st, 1871. The fact mentioned greatly strengthens the position taken above. "*Fossil Bats.*—At the meeting of the British Association, Professor Van Beneden, of Louvain, read a paper on 'The Bats of the Mammoth Period compared with existing species.' The learned Professor, after devoting much study to the remains of species collected in the caves of Belgium, finds that they do not differ in any way from those now existing in the same country."

though so familiar with it, it is not wonderful that he should fail yet more signally in attempting to show that "there is no fundamental difference between man and the higher mammals in their mental faculties." By an unfortunate omission he does not tell us what, in his view, would constitute such a difference. Now, not to refer again to the question as to the difference between reason and instinct, it may be fairly maintained that, whatever mental faculties the higher mammals may possess—even granting that they possess all Mr. Darwin would contend for—if it be the case that man possesses, besides those faculties, other higher mental faculties of which they exhibit not the slightest trace, here we have a difference that is both fundamental and vital. But, on Mr. Darwin's own admission, this is the case. While he fails to show that any one of the lower animals exercises *self-consciousness*, or possesses the power of *abstraction*, or is able to form *general ideas*, or is capable of *progressive improvement*, or has "man's large power of *connecting definite sounds with definite ideas*," he does not omit to tell us that "no one supposes that any one of the lower animals reflects on whence he comes and whither he goes, what is life, and what is death, and so forth." But why do not the lower animals exercise such reflection? Clearly because no one of them possesses those mental powers by which man is able so to reflect. This power of reflection, and of taking action as the result of such reflection, is one of the grand distinguishing characteristics of man. Mr. Darwin thus contradicts himself. He first tells us that "there is no fundamental difference between man and the higher mammals in their mental faculties," and then he points us to where such a difference lies! "Such a difference has no existence," he says; "none whatever;" then, after a vain attempt to throw a veil of mist over the point, it shines out so clearly, even to himself, that he is forced to exclaim, " Lo, here it is, after all !"

This "fundamental difference" appears again in Mr. Darwin's utter failure to show that any one of the lower animals is capable of conceiving the thought of God, of eternity, or of immortality; of exercising the "highly complex feeling of religious devotion," or possessing "the grand idea of God hating sin and loving righteousness." Why does man possess this capacity while all the lower animals are not only entirely destitute of it, but have manifestly no tendency in them to develop it ? There can be but one answer to this question. While man possesses an animal nature, he possesses also a higher nature, endowed with higher faculties, in which none of the lower animals share. Even admitting, then, that some of the inferior animals possess such faculties as Mr. Darwin contends for— imitation, attention, memory, curiosity, wonder, &c.—they are but brute faculties after all. They are the faculties of creatures whose nature is essentially and fundamentally inferior to that of man—faculties, therefore, which can be exercised only on the low and limited level on which the brute lives and moves and has its being. There is thus all the difference in mental faculty between man and the highest of the lower animals, that there is between a nature that is rational and a nature that is irrational ; between a creature that is under a law of force and impulse, and one that is under a law of motive and moral obligation and duty ; a creature limited in its capacity for improvement, and one capable of endless progression ; a creature whose aims and impulses all relate to the body and that cannot possibly conceive the thoughts of God, accountability, retribution, immortality, eternity—and a creature that can derive its motives and aims from unseen spiritual realities, and that can hold high and blessed fellowship with God.

If Mr. Darwin made a mistake in carrying his hypothesis into the domain of mind, he has made a yet greater mistake in carrying it into that of conscience and the moral sense, for, as he himself informs us, this sense is possible only where there is human reason. "Any animal whatever," he says, "endowed with well-marked social instincts would inevitably acquire a moral sense or conscience as soon as its intellectual powers had become as well developed, or nearly as well developed, as in man." But if an animal must thus become an intellectual creature before it can become a moral creature, Mr. Darwin must show that such intellectual development is possible to it, before his argument can have the least weight. As we have just seen, however, he not only fails to show that brute intellect is essentially the same as human intellect, but indicates various points of fundamental difference between them.

I should be justified, therefore, in altogether declining to notice what he says in this part of his subject, and would certainly do so, were it not for the very serious error involved in the views he puts forth, and the very serious consequences that must result should those views find their way into the popular mind. According to Mr. Darwin, conscience is based on the social animal instincts, and is merely the result of their fuller development in an animal in which the mental faculties are being developed as well. But he tells us further that he does "not wish to maintain that every strictly social animal . . . would acquire exactly the same moral sense as ours;" that, "to take an extreme case, if men were reared under precisely the same conditions as hive-bees, there can hardly be a doubt that our unmarried females would think it a sacred duty to kill their brothers, and mothers would strive to kill their fertile daughters; and no one would think of interfering!" What is this but to tell us that there is no stable and unchanging rule of duty; that our notions of right and wrong are merely the result of the conditions under which we have lived, and would, under other conditions, be entirely different from what they are; nay, that we might have been so reared that family murder would be a "sacred duty," and that a mother would be fulfilling her highest moral and social obligations in taking the life of her hapless babe!

It is easy to see how such sentiments may be abused, and how, under the stimulus of such Malthusian notions as Mr. Darwin has imbibed, and on which, indeed, his book is largely based, a more convenient mode of getting rid of our surplus population, or preventing its increase, might be advocated and introduced. Mr. Darwin seems darkly to hint at something of the kind when he tells us how, among "savages, the weak in body and mind are soon eliminated," that is—to express it in plain English—*killed off*, if not by murder, by cruelty and neglect; while those who "survive commonly exhibit a vigorous state of health;" that we civilized men "check the process of elimination" by our asylums, hospitals, poor laws, medical skill, vaccination, &c.; that "thus the weak members of civilized society propagate their kind;" that, "except in the case of man himself, hardly any one is so ignorant as to allow his worst animals to breed;" and that all this is "highly injurious to the race of man!"

Such were formerly the private sentiments of Mr. Darwin. They are now his advanced opinions—the scientific teaching which he offers to the British public—the new and better light which he has discovered by his life-long studies of animal existence, and which he holds up to guide us into a more excellent way. He tells us indeed that "we could not check our sympathy" towards the poor, and weak, and suffering, "without deterioration in the noblest part of our nature;" but what avails such a hint when he puts into the mouths of such as might be disinclined to take it, such a reply as the following to the promptings of any kindly impulses of their nature?—the exercise of them would be "highly injurious to the race of man."

If such sentiments were generally adopted — which, happily, we have little reason to fear—in the course of a few generations they would assuredly open the flood-gates of irreligion and immorality in our land, and cause such an outburst of selfishness and impiety as would overturn our social institutions from their lowest foundations, and introduce a moral disorder and anarchy which might be long in passing away. Such a change has been brought about in France by the working of a false and irrational religion on the one hand, and by the rash speculations of (so-called) philosophers and men of science on the other; and what has occurred in France is possible in England. We cannot reasonably expect a people to be better than the God they believe in. To be like the object of their faith and worship is about as high an ambition as can influence them. Let our countrymen, then, learn to believe in the deity which Mr. Darwin introduces to them—let them discard the God and Redeemer of Christianity for the powers which he tells them have founded and built up the rational world—Natural Selection and Sexual Selection—and what could we expect as the result but the upturning of the foundations of both religion and morality; the destruction of all that is pure, and gentle, and loving, and sympathetic in the relations of life as they at present subsist among us; and the substitution of force, and passion, and cunning, for benevolence and self-restraint. There would then be a case of what Mr. Darwin might regard as "reversion" indeed; civilized men would become civilized savages, and the world would go back into the darkness of the deepest moral night.

I can have no wish to charge Mr. Darwin with atheism, but, certainly, his work now before us, while it speaks of "a Creator and Ruler of the universe," and of the question as to his existence having been "answered in the affirmative by the highest intellects that have ever lived," contains no clear and definite acknowledgment of belief in Him as cherished by Mr. Darwin himself. Practically, Darwinism —as it has been called—in this latest exposition of it, is atheism, and atheism of the most dreary and hopeless kind. If it does not deny God, it ignores God. Its tendency is to remove the Divine Being entirely from the view of man, and to lead to disbelief in his having any connection whatever with, or interest in, human affairs. The world is given up by Him to the hard, conscienceless, unsympathetic power and rule of Natural Selection. There is no beneficent providence.* For anything that God now does in the province of Nature and of man, there might as well be written over it, "No God is here." If man come to have "the idea of a universal and beneficent Creator of the universe," it is not "until he has been elevated by long-continued culture." If "the feeling of religious devotion" inspire man, it is but the result of the development in him of faculties which the lower animals possess as well as himself;—for, "in the deep love of a dog for his master" "we see

In reply to Professor Asa Gray, Mr. Darwin maintains that, although we might wish to find proof that a beneficent providence had guided the evolution of animal forms, we have no evidence that a beneficent providence has done so even in the case of man himself. See the closing sentences of Mr. Darwin's work on "The Variation of Animals and Plants under Domestication."

some distant approach to this state of mind." On Mr. Darwin's hypothesis, Divine benevolence, if it exist at all, has never been exercised towards man; Divine revelation is a fable; man is an inscrutable mystery; he is an enigma, insoluble even by himself; his hope of immortality is a dream!

I must add to what I have said that, in my judgment, Homo himself is not free from error. He seems anxious to uphold "the dogma of separate creations," as Mr. Darwin calls it. But this is not—though Homo seems to think so—a dogma contained in the Bible. I read there, after the formation of the heavens and the earth, of but one separate act of creation, and that has reference to man. Scripture nowhere teaches that the Divine Being created each kind of creature separately. In the first chapter of Genesis He is represented as issuing the command, "Let the waters bring forth abundantly the moving creature that hath life, and fowl that may fly above the earth in the open firmament of heaven." "Let the earth bring forth the living creature after his kind, cattle, and creeping thing, and beast of the earth after his kind: and it was so." Farther light is given in the words, "The Spirit of God moved" (brooded) "upon the face of the waters," as the source and fountain of life. While the inferior creatures are thus summoned into existence by God, man is represented as having been created separately—by himself. We read concerning him, "And the Lord God formed man of the dust of the ground, and breathed into his nostrils the breath of life; and man became a living soul." But no one would understand these words as meaning that the Divine Being appeared visibly upon this earth, and that, taking a handful of its dust, he moulded it into human form, and then breathed into it the spirit of life. All that we can rightly deduce from such language is this: man has derived existence from God; his body was formed by Divine power from the material of the earth which he inhabits; the life inspiring him has come from his Creator. We are told nothing of the forces by which Divine power wrought in building up the material structure of man. Any such reference would have been unsuitable for the time in which those writings were prepared, and for those into whose hands they were first to come. Kingsley has well remarked that, if Scripture had spoken of the material world, and of its creation, in language that would have been unintelligible to early man—and it would have done so, had it spoken in the language of modern science—it could not have spoken of unseen things so as to command his belief.

One expression used in the sacred narrative is worthy of special consideration. Of the various creatures summoned into existence, each is said to be "*after his kind*," words which seem to imply that, from the first, each species was distinct from every other. It was a "*kind*" by itself. There is nothing in the analogy of nature that would lead us to regard such a conclusion as untrue. It is well known that some sixty-four or sixty-five different elements enter into the composition of the inorganic world. Why may it not be supposed then that many different kinds of life have wrought in the building up of the organic world—the world of living things—of plants, and animals, and men? If all the different kinds of matter that exist could be traced to one primordial element, this would give an *a priori* probability to the supposition that all the different kinds of living creatures we see around us have sprung from one primal germ; but, hitherto, chemists have attempted such a reduction of the primary elements of matter in vain. They cannot make out oxygen to be anything other than oxygen, or gold to be anything other than gold. So with the remaining elements; each differs essentially from all the others. Why then may we not suppose the life that animates each species of living creature to be a kind by itself, essentially distinct from every other?

It is true we do not know what life is—that mysterious principle which binds together inorganic elements into organized and living forms. The anatomist cannot take it upon his scalpel, and subject it to examination; but that life exists in different kinds seems evident enough. It will hardly be affirmed that vegetable life is the same in kind with animal life. On what ground then can it be maintained that the life of one species of plant or animal is identical with the life of every other species, and that species differ, not *ab origine*, but merely from development? Such an assertion may be made, but cannot be proved; nor, when we consider more closely, does it appear to wear even the semblance of truth.

It is well known that not only does the blood of man differ from that of any kind of lower animal, but that, so far as examination has been carried, the blood of each species of animal differs from that of every other species. The microscope and chemical analysis clearly reveal this fact. This difference, moreover, is not confined to the blood; it extends to the other fluids and secretions of the body, and also to the minute structures of which it is made up. The farther research is carried, the more numerous and remarkable are these differences found to be.* It is a fact which may be most clearly proved, that, while the different

---

* Those who wish to see the facts here referred to more fully stated and discussed, should consult an able article in *The British Quarterly Review* for October, 1871.

creatures that exist start from germs which no kind of analysis hitherto employed enables us to distinguish from each other; each species, soon after development, begins to diverge from every other on a pathway of its own, forming for itself a different kind of blood, secreting different fluids, weaving different tissues, and, at length, appearing in a different form. In this form it manifests instincts which differ from those of every other species; it manifests different mental qualities, different habits, and different dispositions; at length it dies bequeathing its specific differences to its kind. All the efforts of man to obliterate the peculiarities of any one species, or blend two different species together in permanent union, or originate a new species from a union of two, have signally failed. Species persist, and, so far as appears, always have persisted, in retaining their peculiarities and their essential distinctness, and thus seem to proclaim regarding themselves what is written of them in the record in Genesis: " We are each ' *after his kind.*' "

I may suggest, though I do so with the utmost diffidence, that the primary germs, from which different species have sprung, were originally produced by the " *brooding* of the Spirit of God on the face of the waters," mentioned in Genesis i. 2. These germs lay at first in the womb of the mother earth, potentially the future tribes that were to inherit it. From these germs the various kinds of living creatures were afterwards brought into animate existence by some peculiar exercise of Divine power, into the nature of which it is vain for us to inquire. The account thus given in the sacred narrative is certainly as consistent with the discoveries of modern science as that suggested by Mr. Darwin, when he speaks of " life, with its several powers, as having been originally breathed by the Creator into a few forms, or into one."

The Darwinian notion of man's having had a series of bestial progenitors is certainly irreconcilable with the sacred narrative of Genesis, as it is also with those fundamental ideas of Revelation—the Fall, and the Redemption of Man. Whether it is consistent with any form of religion, I need not here consider; but it is utterly inconsistent with Christianity. I am aware that an attempt has been made to modify Mr. Darwin's hypothesis with respect to man. It has been suggested that, though man's body may have, for the most part, a brutish origin, yet that Divine power may have miraculously interfered to strip it of its hairy covering, to increase the size of the brain, and produce other changes. Such an idea—in itself ridiculous—if it be intended to reconcile Mr. Darwin's hypothesis with Christianity, is useless and futile. Revelation clearly supposes man's pristine, God-derived purity, and the possibility of his being restored to that purity again. It teaches that man was created in the image of God, and that that image may again be impressed on him. Few will deny the possibility of this as to man. It is utterly inconceivable in the case of the brute. I very deeply regret that Mr. Darwin should think otherwise.

I can now have no hesitation in pronouncing the Defendant guilty with respect to the charge made against him by Homo, and, considering the injurious consequences likely to result from Mr. Darwin's statements, I award to the Plaintiff——

Homo. My Lord, will you allow me to say that, as your Lordship has so clearly shown the justness of my cause, and as I am not influenced by any vindictive feeling toward Mr. Darwin, I shall be amply satisfied if he will publish a retractation of the libel, and also of the errors which his book contains.

Lord C. It is not for me to object to such an arrangement. I will therefore defer the award which I was about to make, in order that Mr. Darwin may have time to reconsider the matter, and to frame—as I trust he will—an ample and complete retractation. Should he still continue his studies in Natural History, he will do well henceforth to confine himself to that department in which he has hitherto been so successful. By all means let him go on collecting facts, but let him see that what he records as facts are sufficiently verified. Seeing, however, that his attempts at theorising have been so unsatisfactory, and might lead to such deplorable results, let him now put a restraint on his imagination. I hope he will henceforth take for his motto, the words of one of the most illustrious philosophers which England or the world has ever produced, "NON FINGO HYPOTHESES."

Just Published, Second Edition, with Illustrations,
Price 2s. 6d.

HOMO versus DARWIN:

A JUDICIAL EXAMINATION OF STATEMENTS RECENTLY PUBLISHED BY MR. DARWIN REGARDING

"THE DESCENT OF MAN."

By W. P. LYON, B.A.

LITERARY NOTICES.

An able critic in *The Christian World* of September 15th, 1871, writes:—

"From some previous acquaintance with the subject, I hesitate not to pronounce 'Homo *versus* Darwin' a complete refutation of the assumptions and mischievous speculations of Darwin.'....It is written in a clear and pointed style; is free from technicalities, and adapted to all readers; while it is cast in a dramatic form, that not only relieves the tediousness of discussion, but gives to it singular liveliness and effect."

The Rev. JAMES PARSONS, writing from *Harrogate*, says:—

"With regard to 'Homo,' it is just the thing....The mode of treating 'The Descent of Man' is *precisely right*, and the volume is adapted for great usefulness. It is far more scientific than the book it opposes....I will commend 'Homo' as I have opportunity."

"We strongly commend this small volume to the careful perusal of any whose minds have been occupied by the consideration of Mr. Darwin's absurd theories. The book will be found to be full of wit and wisdom. The summing up of the judge at the end of the trial contains a good compendium of the whole case. We hope that, amongst our intelligent young people, it will have an extensive circulation."—*The Watchman.*

"The work is written in a somewhat humorous strain, but the writer never loses sight of the gravity of the questions discussed. His remarks on the bearing of the subject on Christian truth are most important. We can cordially recommend this little volume, and hope it may circulate wherever Mr. Darwin's views have met with any degree of acceptance."—*The Record.*

"The argument is very cleverly conducted, and is the best assault we have seen on Mr. Darwin's system."—*The Graphic.*

"The facts and fictions so ingeniously wrought up together in Darwin's work are here, sometimes playfully, at other times more seriously, untwisted, and the indubitable facts of natural science separated from the fallacious hypothesis sought to be drawn from them. We heartily commend this little volume to all who are interested in the question."—*Edinburgh Daily Review.*

"The author has discussed Darwinism in a way which is not only conclusive in argument, but which awakens and sustains the interest of the reader from first to last."—*Christian Witness*.

"The writer of this little volume brings logic, scientific knowledge, and wit to bear in the exposition of Mr. Darwin's fallacies, and supplies an admirable refutation of his theories."—*Evangelical Magazine*.

"We cannot well over-rate the value of this trenchant and decisive exposure of Mr. Darwin's plausible sophistries....The writer limits himself to a remarkably clear and conclusive investigation of Mr. Darwin's principles in the light of common sense. He exposes the looseness of his logic, the assumptions of his alleged facts, the incompleteness of his inductions, and the invalidity of his conclusions, in a style which is as cheerful to read as the matter is instructive."—*Church Opinion*.

"The author may fairly be congratulated on the ability he has brought to bear on his subject, and his defence of the theory respecting the origin of man, usually based on the teaching of the Scriptures."—*London City Press*.

"This *brochure* takes the form of an arbitration inquiry, to decide according to rules acknowledged in English judicature, how far Mr. Darwin has established his hypothesis, which the plaintiff denounces as a libel on human nature—namely, that man is remotely descended from a hairy quadruped, furnished with a tail, pointed ears, and great canine teeth; such quadruped having, in the course of unnumbered ages, been developed from a small marine creature, now found clinging to rocks, and consisting of 'a simple, tough, leathery sac, with two small projecting orifices.' Representations of Mr. Darwin's patriarch, and of his alleged near relation, the gorilla, are brought into court to illustrate the question at issue. Six days are supposed to be devoted to the inquiry, the first of which is occupied with the plaintiff's case, and the last with the summing up of the arbitrator; the intermediate days are devoted to the defence, which consists of extracts from Mr. Darwin's published works, in explanation of the grounds upon which he rests his theory; these are interspersed with free comments by Homo, pointing out the deficient links in this chain of reasoning....Homo very fairly exposes the pitiful straits into which the theories of 'natural selection,' 'sexual selection,' *et hoc genus omne*, infallibly lead their propounders....The line of demarcation between the mental powers of men and other animals is very markedly brought out. Those who have not time to wade through more elaborate tomes will find the points at issue fairly set forth, and in a very readable form, in this little volume."—*The Literary World*.

"This work discusses, with marked ability, from a popular point of view, the well-known opinions of Mr. Darwin regarding the descent of Man."—*School Board Chronicle*.

"A popular exposure of the fallacies of Darwin....So long as weak minds obsequiously bow before the Baal theories of the hour, there will be need of Elijahs to mock them. Here wit and argument are blended. The work speaks for itself."—*The Sword and Trowel*.

"This work dispels the Darwinian fallacies with a good deal of acuteness, and will be perused with pleasure."—*Bristol Mercury*.

London: Hamilton, Adams, & Co., 32, Paternoster Row.
And all Booksellers.

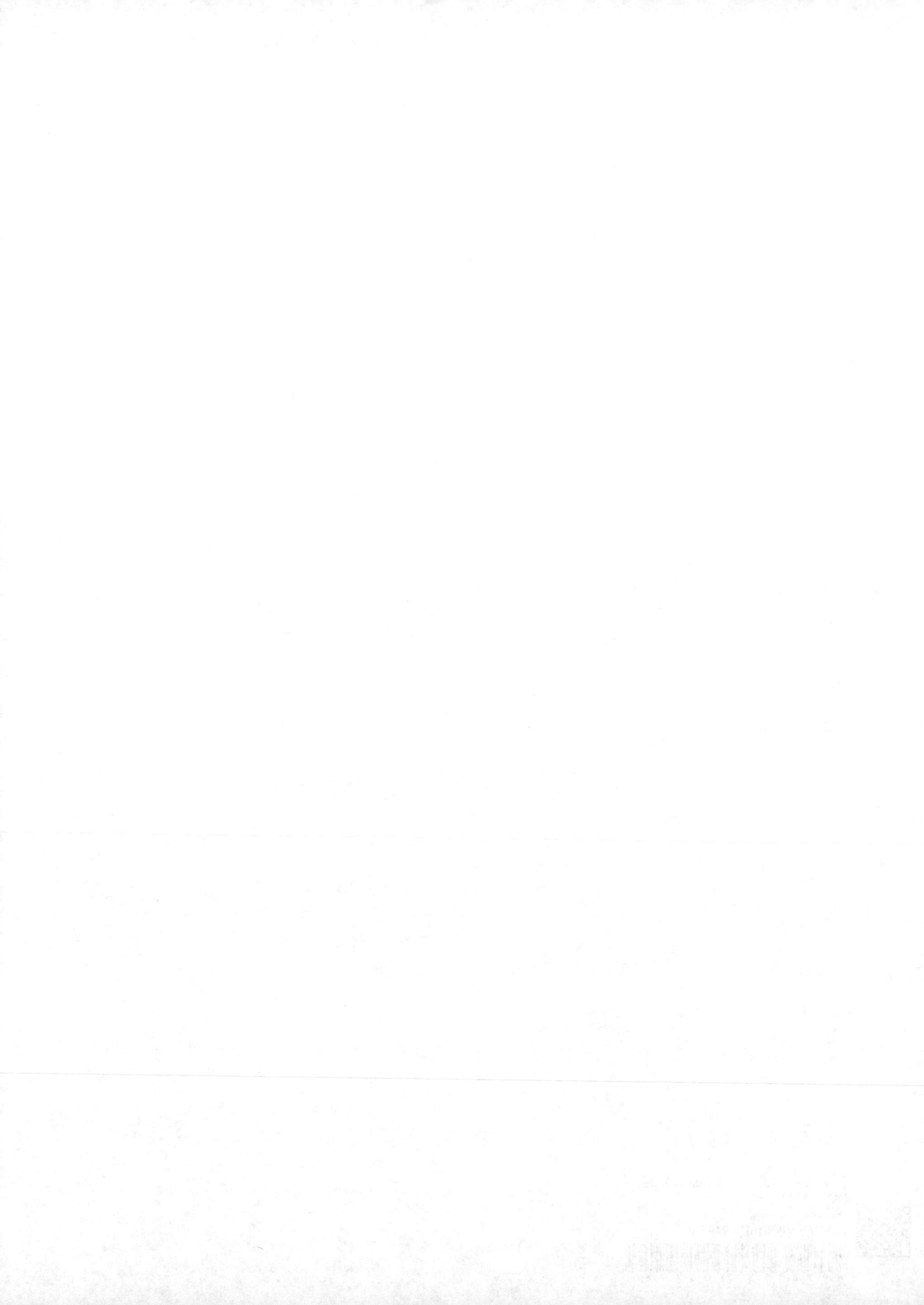

www.ingramcontent.com/pod-product-compliance
Lightning Source LLC
LaVergne TN
LVHW061215060426
835507LV00016B/1949